7 Myths about Christianity

DALE & SANDY LARSEN

InterVarsity Press
Downers Grove, Illinois

InterVarsity Press
P.O. Box 1400, Downers Grove, IL 60515
World Wide Web: www.ivpress.com
E-mail: mail@ivpress.com

InterVarsity Press® is the book-publishing division of InterVarsity Christian Fellowship/USA®, a student movement active on campus at hundreds of universities, colleges and schools of nursing in the United States of America, and a member movement of the International Fellowship of Evangelical Students. For information about local and regional activities, write Public Relations Dept., InterVarsity Christian Fellowship/USA, 6400 Schroeder Rd., P.O. Box 7895, Madison, WI 53707-7895.

All Scripture quotations, unless otherwise indicated, are taken from the Holy Bible, New International Version®. NIV®. *Copyright ©1973, 1978, 1984 by International Bible Society. Used by permission of Zondervan Publishing House. All rights reserved.*

Cover photograph: Tony Stone Images

ISBN 0-8308-1909-6

Printed in the United States of America ♾

Library of Congress Cataloging-in-Publication Data

Larsen, Dale.
  Seven myths about Chritianity / Dale and Sandy Larsen.
    p.   cm.
  Includes bibliographical references.
  ISBN 0-8308-1909-6 (pbk. : alk. paper)
  1. Apologetics. I. Larsen, Sandy. II. Title.
BT1102.L275 1998
239—dc21   98-14178
                                                                                     CIP

20	19	18	17	16	15	14	13	12	11	10	9	8	7	6	5	4	3	2	1
15	14	13	12	11	10	09	08	07	06	05	04	03	02	01	00	99	98		

Introduction

It all started with a conversation with some Christian students at a small private college.

The school, historically connected with a church, has in the past twenty or so years abandoned Christian faith as the center of its purpose. In class these students had been hearing Christianity put down and blamed for many of the world's problems, including the pollution of the planet and the ruin of indigenous cultures.

One Thanksgiving Day, sitting in our living room among the debris of pie plates and Pictionary, the students talked about what their professors and fellow students were saying. Remarkably, they took the anti-Christian criticisms at face value. They were willing to let the faith which they professed take the blame for victimizing the world. They had also accepted the idea that while their Christian faith worked for them personally, other faiths were just as good if they worked for other people.

The students' responses moved us to explore some of those chronic gripes against Christianity. In this book we choose to call them "myths," using "myth" in the most popular sense: something commonly believed and repeated but seldom examined to see if it is fact. We chose seven, knowing we could have chosen others and could have chosen many more than seven.

The accusations in this book's table of contents may have come from your own mouth or smoldered in your own mind. Maybe you've walked away from the church because you couldn't handle the narrowness and insensitivity you found there. Maybe you're fed up with Christians who hold absolute opinions but have no idea what they're talking about and seem to come from another century, if not another planet.

Or maybe you've been hurt by hearing yourself, your faith and your fellow believers negatively stereotyped. In the face of half-truths you wish for a way to defend yourself and your beliefs. You want to persuade people who have walked away from the faith that they are walking away from a parody of true Christianity.

Each of these seven myths has an element of truth in it, or else the myth would never have gotten started. Christians have been and are guilty of each of these seven failings and many others. Our purpose is not to defend or excuse the sins of any Christians, including ourselves. When we use the term *Christianity* in this book we do not mean "the established church" or "a religion" or "Christian people in general." We mean Christianity's essence, the authentic way of Jesus as he meant it to be—the real thing.

As committed Christians the authors can never be purely objective about these seven stereotypes. We have tried to be as fair as our own admittedly pro-Christian bias will allow. In that spirit of combined idealism and realism, we will be grateful for every reader who approaches these seven myths with a genuinely open mind.

1/ "Christians Force Their Morality on Others"

MYTH #1: "Christians are judgmental. They act as society's moral watchdogs, and they try to censor everything from the arts to sex education."

Amanda: Do you realize we're living in sin?
Elyot: Not according to the Catholics. Catholics don't recognise divorce. We're
*   married as much as ever we were.*
Amanda: Yes, dear, but we're not Catholics.
Elyot: Never mind, it's nice to think they'd sort of back us up.
—a couple divorced 5 years, meeting again on their respective honeymoons and
sneaking away from their new spouses, in Noel Coward's "Private Lives"

AIDS educators called it censorship. A condom distribution plan in New York City high schools was restrained when the school board wanted more emphasis on abstinence. One AIDS-prevention worker complained, "We're talking life and death. We can't submit our work to the sex police."[1]

Defensive words. That AIDS worker saw her vital lifesaving effort about to be torpedoed.

Let the "sex police" come armed with the moral force of religion, and the torpedo looks more like an H-bomb.

Why Do You Want to Know?

Our local newspaper was running a series of pro-and-con articles on controversial issues and asked us to write an evaluation of the Human Growth and Development (sex education) curriculum in the local schools. It wasn't clear whether they expected us to be "pro" or "con," but we dived into the project. As advisors for our church's middle-school youth group, we had heard the students talk about carrying eggs around for a week to simulate caring for an infant. Some Christian parents had expressed doubts about the curriculum. We were curious to see and judge it firsthand.

After two weeks of research, the most enlightening piece of information we had turned up was a copy of the state law saying: "The school board shall make the complete human growth and development curriculum and all instructional materials available upon request for inspection at any time."[2] On the subject of the curriculum itself we got mostly runarounds and wild goose chases.

The curriculum director gave us outlines of curriculum objectives and referred us to the teachers. The middle-school teacher was cautiously cooperative; the high-school teachers drew back in suspicion. Their eyes got cold, their posture stiff. "Why do you want to know?" they demanded. Explaining that the newspaper had sent us didn't help. The teachers sent us back to the curriculum director, who sent us back to the teachers, who sent us to the principal, all of them clearly praying that we would go away.

We didn't. When we had finally pried the curriculum out of reluctant hands and the project was done, Sandy remarked: "I didn't learn anything about sex, but I sure learned a lot about the school system."

Under Attack by the Values-Pushers

Several teachers eventually opened up to us and explained that the sex-education curriculum had been "attacked by people who want to push their values on others." Suddenly all the stonewalling made sense. There were some grounds for defensiveness (though not enough grounds for two weeks of runarounds). We heard that public forums had been held to discuss the Human Growth and Development program. Some vocal Christians had come to criticize the curriculum and insist on an alternative of their choosing.

Behind the teachers' defensiveness lay fear and hurt. They wanted to keep kids from dying of AIDS and keep teen girls from short-circuiting their lives through pregnancy. They thought their curriculum was doing that. Now their lifesaving work was being threatened by religious zealots.

Moral Crusaders

Sex education isn't the only place where Christians are seen as pushing their morality on others. Christians seem to think they're right and everybody else is wrong about all kinds of moral issues. When other people don't see the light, instead of respecting others' freedom to choose, Christians charge in—or weasel in—and try to manipulate public policy to make sure their agenda wins.

Certain people who identify themselves as Christians have even resorted to very non-Christian violence. An anti-abortion protester shoots a doctor dead at a Florida abortion clinic. The shooter shows no remorse. Convicted of murder, he says he was doing God's will.

If most Christians aren't that violent, they can at least be sneaky. Critics say that conservative Christians run for school boards while keeping their religious agenda under wraps. Once in power, they trample on diversity by imposing their narrow views on the public schools. A couple of recent examples:

In Florida's Lake County district, crucial school-board decisions about construction projects were held up while a Christian-right majority formulated, then adopted, an "America First" policy instructing teachers to promote American values as "superior to other foreign or historic cultures."

In Vista, California, near San Diego, board meetings turned into all-night shoutfests when a Christian-right majority promoted use of a creationism textbook.[3]

Some Christians have gained a reputation as self-appointed censors for what everybody else enjoys for entertainment. Rev. Donald Wildmon's American Family Association takes on itself the task of "promoting the Biblical ethic of decency in American society with emphasis on TV," despite the fact that American TV viewers have never invited the AFA to do anything of the kind. Wielding emotion and a strong mailing list,

Wildmon uses the economic power of the boycott to bully companies into withdrawing sponsorship of programs he considers immoral. What's alarming, said *TV Guide*, "is the fact that a single individual with extremely personal views can have such a long reach."[4]

A Set of Moral Guideposts

Not everyone has a problem with the certitude of Christian morality. For a generation who threw away their moral anchors, and for their children who grew up being told there is no absolute right or wrong, the moral compass of Christianity can appear not as a threat but as a desperately needed promise of stability.

The play dialogue which heads this chapter comes from 1930, but the longing expressed is contemporary. We all share Elyot's need to be right. We hunger to be given moral validation, not only deep in our private consciences but by the world outside ourselves. We want to know that we're okay, that our lives somehow square with the way things are supposed to be.

A newspaper article tells of a Cincinnati couple in their late twenties who belong to a flourishing new church. There they find a community which "shares their young adult sensibilities. On Sunday mornings, there is Starbucks coffee that you can carry into the service, MTV-inspired videos that explore the values people live by, and live Christian rock." But the church's appeal goes beyond its twentysomething amenities.

There is all this and there is, for those who want it, the ultimate prize: a set of moral guideposts that point the way to goodness—apparent absolutes in a world in which very little seems absolute anymore.[5]

Few are offended when Christians follow a personal, private "set of moral guideposts." It's when we go public that we run into righteous indignation such as the authors found in our school system.

One of Those Stringy Black Ties

Christians get scary when we go on a crusade (overt or covert) to seize power and rewrite the laws. And it seems Christians are always on one moral crusade or another: to control which books students read in public schools; to shape what people see on television; to keep women from having abortions; to shut down adult bookstores; to ban homosexual marriage; to keep kids from listening to certain music; to cut off public funding for certain kinds of artistic expression. That's when we get accused of pushing our values on others—not to mention being narrow-minded, loud-mouthed bigots, stuck in an idealized past, out of touch with reality, having no idea of the depth or complexity of the issues and no appreciation for diversity.

Writing for the liberal magazine *The New Republic,* Michael Lewis spent several days in 1996 shadowing Pastor Ted Haggard of Colorado Springs, the current nerve center for Christian activist groups. In his resultant article Lewis was good-natured but mystified: how can intelligent people believe these things that Christians believe? He also observed Pastor Haggard being stereotyped by other reporters, who expected him to "froth at the mouth."

"ABC came here a while ago," [Pastor Haggard] says, "and they really needed to have me be the guy who wanted to take control of the school system. They were hoping to find a guy dressed in black with one of those stringy black ties. When they saw me and I gave them my answers I could see they were disappointed. They ended up finding a guy in Pennsylvania."[6]

Like Pastor Haggard, most Christians can take in stride the accusations of narrow-mindedness or pushiness. What hurts—because we know it's often true—is being accused of lacking the compassion which marked the life of our Lord.

Compassion or Condemnation?

Why do Christians so often come across as condemning, rigid and loveless when we get involved in public disputes? Sometimes it's because we see people about to drive over a cliff and think they need moral confrontation more than they need comfort.

Sometimes it's because we actually are condemning, rigid and loveless.

Shortly before the 1994 election, when activist Christians helped the

Republican Party regain control of Congress, John B. Judis raised some
pointed questions about politics and Christian love:

> The Christian awakenings, beginning in the 1750s, have played an
> immensely positive role in shaping America's transition from colony
> to nation, from agricultural to industrial society—and in lending
> urgency to the struggle against slavery and racial inequality.
>
> Is today's religious right injecting a Christian spirit of compassion
> and selflessness into American politics? The only group that seems to
> elicit its compassion is the unborn; it does not display similar compas-
> sion, for instance, toward the poor or the victims of AIDS—two
> obvious groups for which a modern-day Christian might be expected
> to express concern.[7]

There *are* Christians working with AIDS patients and the poor. One
well-known Christian effort to relieve homelessness is Habitat for Humanity, supported from its earliest days by former U.S. President Jimmy
Carter. Carter was probably the most outspokenly Christian president of
the twentieth century, certainly the one with the sharpest sense that his
Christian faith and morals went *against* the grain of the prevailing culture.
There are many other lower-profile humanitarian efforts by Christians.
Still, John Judis's criticism of Christian lovelessness cuts too close to
home to be discounted.

Planks and Sawdust

Here we should mention something not generally known among nonbelievers: Christians use the club of moral rightness on each other as much
as on outsiders.

The Pilgrims came to North America to escape religious persecution,
but before long they had their own set of social norms, strictly enforced.
After the Civil War, according to church historian Sydney E. Ahlstrom,
churches sidestepped sticky issues like racial segregation and industrial-
ism, preferring to concentrate on the evils of "dancing, tobacco, alcoholic
beverages, gambling, card playing and theatergoing"[8]—taboos still strong
in the memories of American Christians who grew up in the forties and
fifties, and even for some who are younger.

Pickiness about externals has always been a convenient way for Christians to dodge their own inner failings. When Jesus' followers were still just a few people in Palestine, he was already speaking out about the tendency to excuse one's own faults and condemn fellow believers:

Why do you look at the speck of sawdust in your brother's eye and pay no attention to the plank in your own eye? How can you say to your brother, "Let me take the speck out of your eye," when all the time there is a plank in your own eye? You hypocrite, first take the plank out of your own eye, and then you will see clearly to remove the speck from your brother's eye. (Mt 7:3-5)

Morality or Life and Death?

Some people insist that our society's problems are so urgent that we must not waste time talking about moral abstractions. Joseph Fernandez, chancellor of the New York City schools, had this to say about distributing condoms to teenagers: "This is not an issue of morality. It is a matter of life and death."[9]

Certainly it's easier to put things in terms of life and death than to get into the morass of what's right or wrong. If you're alive, you're alive, and if you're dead, you're dead. As for what's right or wrong, who can say anymore? Anyway, if you're dead, what difference does it make? Better to admit that nobody can know and get on with the practicalities of saving lives.

Christians are both amused and angered at how a society of supposedly fluid morals, a society that refuses to agree on standards of right and wrong, can turn so condemning when its ideas are challenged by Christians. "You have a judgmental God," my friend announced to me—not realizing, or maybe not caring, that she was judging my God.

Such supposedly nonjudgmental condemnation equals moral confusion. People wind up making absolute statements about standards of tolerance while denying that any absolute standards exist. George Will and others have called it "cognitive dissonance"—"the condition of minds stocked with starkly incompatible ideas and desires."[10] Abortion on demand is good because it empowers women, except where women choose to selectively abort unwanted girl babies, in which case it is femicide.[11] Censorship of the internet is dictatorship, except when it targets neo-Nazi hate speech or violent fantasies about real women, in which case censorship is a weapon against racism and sexism.[12] Pornography is freedom of speech as long as it's kept from children, except when it degrades women, in which case it is exploitative, unless the women participate willingly because they are proud of their bodies, in which case it is empowering.

Other examples: We must stop the abuse of women; at the same time we must protect the right of music groups to fuel the erotic power fantasies of adolescent males.[13] Free speech is good except when it creates a hostile learning environment in the university classroom, where students should be protected from discomfiting racist or sexist ideas; but protection from discomfort does not extend to devoutly religious students, such as five Orthodox Jewish freshmen at Yale who were forced—against their be-liefs—to live in dorms which one characterized as "the biblical descrip-tion of Sodom and Gomorrah."[14]

Censorship or Remodeling?
In some cases one person's censorship is another person's remodeling job.

During Banned Books Week several years ago, our local librarian wrote a newspaper article decrying censorship and book-banning. The library had just undergone remodeling, and when it was done, several publications had disappeared from the shelves: the magazines *Christian-ity Today, Moody Monthly* (from Moody Bible Institute) and *Christian Century,* and the classic reference work *Interpreter's Dictionary of the Bible.* We were amazed that publications from the full range of conserva-tive, moderate and liberal Christian thought had all been dumped out. Besides, we needed them for our work. When we asked the librarian what had happened, his only explanation was that the library needed more space.

It turns out Christians aren't the only ones who wish everybody else would see the light. *All* people who believe strongly in their own ideas want to see those ideas become dominant in society. If they have the power, they won't hesitate to take things off library shelves when they disagree with what's in them. If they personally lack the power, they will look for ways to force others to take action. Despite all our culture's talk of tolerance, there's a war going on over whose values will have the final say.

In this war all sides have a take-no-prisoners attitude. "Neither side will allow anyone to remain neutral in the culture war. That is why the middle is disappearing. And that is why the culture war is so heated and why compromise is impossible."[15]

Nobody Smiles Like That Anymore

In the past decade, as the war over "values" has eaten up miles of print space, we have noticed an interesting pattern in secular magazines taking on the subject. Their articles tell us it's futile to evoke the values of the past—specifically the 1950s-era values of "Ozzie and Harriet," "Father Knows Best" and "Leave it to Beaver," the values with which the parents of today's teens and college students were raised. Those values, they say, no longer work for today's morally chaotic world.

As a sort of proof, the articles come accompanied by black-and-white photos of intact families from 1950s television programs or ads. The photos are there not to illustrate an ideal but to serve as artifacts from another universe. The people look anachronistic not because of their clothes or hairstyles but because they look so happy. Everybody knows families don't smile like that anymore.

By gymnastics of circular reasoning, the writers tell us we can't possibly return to such naive values because the problems of today's society are too complex and overwhelming. What are those problems? Teen pregnancy, rampant divorce, sexually transmitted diseases, absent fathers, one-parent households, sexual cheapening and exploitation in media, racial conflict, media violence, gang violence, kids who kill without remorse . . . the appalling list goes on.

The list mystifies and frustrates Christians, because these are exactly the problems which a commitment to biblical morality would solve or at least ease. These are problems that escalated just when our society abandoned Christian morals. The coincidence is too big to ignore.

Let's consider one of the most basic biblical standards, chastity before marriage. (It does not belong exclusively to Christianity but occurs in all the great world religions. People who promote abstinence, however, get branded as "the religious right," meaning fundamentalist Christian.) For now let's think of chastity in relation to unmarried teenagers. The problems chastity prevents are exactly the problems all of us—from the most fundamentalist Christian to the most skeptical atheist—would do anything to solve. Teen pregnancy. Sexually transmitted diseases. Young women short-circuiting their futures and young men walking away from responsibility.

Why is there such resistance to teaching chastity when it would accomplish precisely what we all long to see in the lives of young people? Because it's a "religious" value? Religion does not need to play any part in teaching it. Because teenagers are such slaves of their hormones that they can't say no to sex? That's not only insulting to teens, it calls into question every other school program which tells them to say no to drugs, drunk driving, racial slurs, smoking or any other negative behavior.

More in Common Than They Know
Christians are impatient with the circular reasoning that morals won't work because society lacks morals. We resonate with George Will's haunting question: "What can prevent the crumbling of the thin, brittle crust of civilization when the culture itself is assaulting that crust?"[16] With the stakes so high, Christians who jump into the public-policy-setting realm can get strident and, yes, pushy. It turns out we're a lot like those teachers and administrators in our high school who got defensive about their sex-education program.

Those teachers and administrators from whom we worked for two weeks to pry that curriculum were convinced they had the right answers. They didn't want anybody interfering with their program. They were protecting it from criticism. As far as they legally could, they were forcing their values into a place of prominence in the schools despite questions raised by concerned Christian parents. If they and those parents had just sat down together and talked, they might have understood each other. They had more in common than they knew.

A World That Never Was?

Another common indictment of "fifties values," besides the fact that they won't work in today's culture, is that they represent a world which was never real except for a small privileged segment of society.

When Norman Rockwell died, we frequently heard that "he painted an America which never existed." The statement was cynical—and surprisingly provincial. Rockwell's *Saturday Evening Post* covers looked exactly like the places and people a lot of us grew up with. What's more, they looked like them when the magazine came in our mail fresh off the press, not through a haze of nostalgia but while we were growing up. Some who never experienced that world are strangely threatened by it and would prefer to believe it never existed.

David Blankenhorn of the Institute for American Values uses a photograph of the classic, pluperfect fifties family having a barbecue on the beach as a Rorschach test. "Members of the media and academic elites look at the photo and laugh," he says. "They say things like 'That's what I've been fighting against all my life.' But most other people look at it wistfully. One woman said, 'I know the "Ozzie and Harriet" stuff is impossible, but I miss the familyness of it.'"[17]

Why would someone say of the image of a happy family, "That's what I've been fighting against all my life?" Without knowing who said it or the tone of voice or what else was said, we can't explain the statement, but it's certainly far from a culturally inclusive or open-minded comment.

A Time of Hypocrisy?

A more solid criticism of fifties morality, one which deserves more attention, is that the era wasn't as good underneath as it looked on the exterior. The fact that the era's values are called "traditional values" tells us there was a time when such values were held in common, but the era also included moral hypocrisy. The surface perfection of Ozzie and Harriet was too good to be true. Behind the superficial smiles, the men were cruel or distant to their wives and children, the women were trapped and stifled in their stereotyped roles, couples hung on in loveless marriages because divorce was shameful.

Maxine Schnall's book *Limits* claims that no decade has given us a sufficient value system, but about the fifties she makes the case that it was a time when traditional values were actually *abandoned:*

Both the "glad-handing" husband and the "happy homemaker" wife quickly shed their inner code of personal limits—the traditional values drummed into them by their parents, their schoolteachers, the church, the government—in order to gain the approval of their group.[18]

Having been there, we believe there was a general moral consensus in 1950s America. What was fading, however, was the *reason* for the morals people lived by. Most people agreed that certain things were right and certain things were wrong, but they were beginning to lose track of why those things were or had ever been right and wrong.

The argument that the morality of the fifties was only hypocrisy becomes then actually an argument to return to the "traditional values" which were abandoned. The word *hypocrite,* which Jesus used frequently in his accusations of religious people, comes from the theatrical world and has to do with the masks worn by actors.

[I]t was a custom for Greek and Roman actors to speak in large masks with mechanical devices for augmenting the force of the voice; hence the word became used metaphorically of a dissembler, a hypocrite.[19]

Many Americans in the fifties were living on the memory of earlier spiritual renewal. Their behavior was externally compliant, but it no longer sprang from deep sources of personal conviction. The further people get from true spiritual renewal, the more their morals become detached from the internal spiritual life and the more superficial they become. Without a basis in reason—a "why?"—morality becomes a mask, something artificial applied to the surface. It may convince observers, but it says nothing about the real person beneath.

The good thing about hypocrisy is that hypocrites agree there is something good they ought to look as if they're doing. The bad thing is that they have no reason for doing it other than looking good.

The New Orthodoxy
Charles Colson was a man who didn't even bother to carry on the external

trappings of hypocrisy. In the Nixon White House he was famous for living by a ruthlessly utilitarian standard of doing whatever worked. When Colson came to the end of himself, he came to Christ. Through Prison Fellowship and Justice Fellowship he now works for reform of the legal system and spiritual renewal of prisoners. Colson's perspective is interesting because he has been on both extremes of the moral issue:

> So often nonbelievers disdain us as anachronists clinging to an ancient orthodoxy with no relevance for the modern world. Well, it is far better to cling to an ancient orthodoxy, with its firm standard of truth, than to claim no orthodoxy at all, yet still act as if you have one.[20]

The new orthodoxy is "tolerance," in Colson's words "redefined as the freedom to choose from a smorgasbord of morally equivalent lifestyles—homosexuality, adultery, premarital promiscuity. Take your pick. . . . And this smorgasbord-style tolerance, *itself a moral position,* tramples on the sensibilities of any who hold to moral absolutes—particularly Christians."[21]

Values As Devices

Tolerance as a virtue had its early champions in the "values clarification" movement in education in the early 1970s. Proponents Merrill Harmin and Sidney B. Simon explained why "moralizing" did not work: because young people were "bombarded with different, and often contradictory, sets of values."

> We have tried to teach values. But in a world of confusion and conflict about values, this is not enough. No matter how sincere we may be in our desire to help, all we leave the young person with is one more input, one more moralizing message, which goes into his overloaded computer to be processed along with others.[22]

Teachers therefore had three alternative ways to develop values in young people:

> One alternative is to do nothing about such development. Another is to transmit a pre-existing set of values to students. A third is to help students find their own values.[23]

Harmin and Simon opted for the third alternative. They proposed two possible ways for students to find their own values. One was "the clarifying liberal arts approach," exposing students to the best their culture has to offer; the authors quickly dismissed that idea as impractical. Instead they went for "the values skills approach." In neither case, they reassured us, are values to be taken as objective or absolute.

> The main task of these approaches is not to identify and transmit the "right" values, but to help a student clarify his own values so he can obtain the values that best suit him and his environment, so he can adjust himself to a changing world, and so he can play an intelligent role in influencing the way the world changes.[24]

Anyone who has taught young adolescents knows that doing a values clarification exercise is only slightly safer than walking into a mine field. Everything depends on students listening and accepting each other with no snickering and no condemnation—a challenge even for polite adults and a superhuman moral feat for junior highers.

Harmin and Simon admitted that teachers had two problems: they had to avoid "promoting particular values" and they had to "devise methods of controlling behavior" to keep young people from devastating each other emotionally in class. "The usual solution here," they said, "is to have behavior rules that are not defended as values, but merely as devices for protecting individuals and groups against pressures from others."[25]

Renaming values as "devices" did not change what they were, and enforcing those "devices" was itself teaching values. The fluid moral standard set by values clarification turned out to be something its teachers could not consistently live with themselves. Rather than teaching moral absolutes openly and explicitly, they ended up—knowingly or unknowingly—teaching absolutes as an underlying part of the curriculum.

Diversity Is Fun
The virtue of tolerance flourishes on university campuses, where it takes the form of a dynamic movement to understand and appreciate many diverse cultures.

> Although "multiculturalism" has taken a lot of flak from Christians, we should say that we (the authors) have a longtime habit of actively mixing and learning about various cultures. We keep in touch with

international students on our local U. of Minnesota campus; they celebrate our holidays with us, and they come to our home and cook their ethnic meals. For six years we were a volunteer host family for international graduate students at Northwestern University (through International Students, Inc.). During our three years overseas we lived anything but a tourist lifestyle. Look around our home and you'll see items from Ukraine, Sweden, Japan, mainland China, England, Israel, India, Northern Ireland, Scotland—things gotten in those places or given to us by international friends.

A few days ago we were touched by a truly multicultural e-mail message from a student who signed himself "a very very proud Bangladeshi." His home country was once under the dominion of the British Empire. He has every reason to resent the British. Yet he was bursting with pride that Bangladesh had just qualified for the World Cup, not in soccer but in that most British of all sports—cricket!

True multiculturalism is not only fun, it promotes genuine human understanding and empathy. We agree with Barbara Ehrenreich's cautions:

> I—along with so many educated white people of my generation—was a victim of monoculturalism. . . . The culture that we studied was, in fact, one culture and, from a world perspective, all too limited and ingrown. Diversity is challenging, but those of us who have seen the alternative know it is also richer, livelier and ultimately more fun.[26]

Because we enjoy mixing diverse cultures, it disappoints us that "multiculturalism" often stifles discussion and distorts cultural understanding.

Even Lake Wobegon Wouldn't Be Funny

Last December our bank, wanting to wish customers a Merry Christmas but not wanting to offend anybody, put up posters sprinkled with symbols of Christmas, Hanukkah, Kwanzaa and probably some other holidays. In the middle of the symbols was the not-very-heartwarming message "Celebrate Diversity!"

There is a good reason why nobody wishes anybody "Happy Diversity!" People who really appreciate a multitude of cultures do not celebrate diversity in itself; they celebrate the unique features of each culture. The self-contradiction in multiculturalism is that what makes each individual culture so strong, fascinating and valuable is precisely the specific narrow worldview of each. The unique customs and traditions of each culture, vigorously celebrated in multiculturalism, would disappear if each culture actually adopted multiculturalism. Without the narrowness of monoculture, even Garrison Keillor's stories of Lake Wobegon would not be funny.

Richard Bernstein served as a correspondent in Hong Kong and Beijing for *Time* and as Paris bureau chief and U.N. bureau chief for the *New York Times*. From his years of experience in other cultures he writes:

> Multiculturalism is a movement of the left, emerging from the counterculture of the 1960s. But culture is powerfully conservative. Culture is what enforces obedience to authority, the authority of parents, of history, of custom, of superstition. Deep attachment to culture is one of the things that prevents different people from understanding one another. . . .
>
> The reality of culture is something that ideological multiculturalists would despise, if they knew what it was. The power of culture, especially the culture rooted in ancient traditions, is anathema to the actual goals and ideology of multiculturalism.[27]

The Monocultural Village

In downtown Duluth there's a store called "Global Village" selling clothes from all over the world. A global village, we are told, is where we all now live. We are also told that it takes a village to raise a child, meaning that children need the support of the entire diverse community in order to grow up healthy and whole.

The contradiction is that there is no such thing as a multicultural village. A real-life village is profoundly *monocultural*. Everyone in a true traditional village society shares one narrow worldview, which is carefully taught to the children the village raises. A village keeps its traditions strong by protecting its children from the influences of other cultures.

Ask a Christian missionary what happens to a real-life villager who converts to Christianity from the accepted native religion. Tolerance? A celebration of multiculturalism? Hardly. The new convert is suspected, ostracized, threatened, perhaps exiled or even killed. In a real village there is no room for diversity.

Striking at the Grand Prejudice

In truth "multiculturalism" does not aim to promote all cultures but to strike a blow at a particular culture which has been dominant in Western society and has sought to dominate the rest of the world.

> The goal [of multiculturalism] is to eliminate prejudice, not just of the petty sort that shows up on sophomore dorm walls, but the grand prejudice that has ruled American universities since their founding: that the intellectual tradition of Western Europe occupies the central place in the history of civilization. . . . This agenda is broadly shared by most organizations of minority students, feminists and gays. It is also the program of a generation of campus radicals who grew up in the '60s and are now achieving positions of academic influence.[28]

Choosing less charitable words to describe those in academic power, George Will made the point that values on campus are increasingly imposed against students' will:

> These tenured radicals, often 1960s retreads, are inverting a 1960s demand. Then students demanded that universities loosen restrictions. Today's radicalism-from-above uses administrative power to impose an improved "consciousness" on students.[29]

Like earlier cultural imperialists, promoters of multiculturalism see the world through narrowed eyes. They begin by looking for support for what they already know is true, and they have to overlook a lot of data that doesn't fit their premise. For example, the traditional societies which multiculturalism celebrates are often narrow about race and sex. Dinesh D'Souza, the Indian-born scholar regarded as either the hero or the villain of the multicultural issue on campus, makes this ironic point:

> [B]y and large, non-Western cultures have no developed tradition of racial equality. Not only do they violate equality in practice, but the very principle is alien to them, regarded by many with suspicion and contempt.

Moreover, many of these cultures have deeply ingrained ideas of male superiority. . . . Feminism is simply not indigenous to non-Western cultures.[30]

Who's in Power?

"What is distressing," wrote Jerry Adler, "is that at the university, of all places, tolerance has to be imposed rather than taught, and that 'progress' so often is just the replacement of one repressive orthodoxy by another."[31]

Over a quarter of a century ago, dealing with a student generation who were waging their own culture war against the establishment, Francis Schaeffer predicted our current situation. He said then that it would make no difference whether the student radicals or the establishment won. Because neither side was operating from an objective moral basis, whichever one prevailed would enforce its will by power.

Whether it is a Left Wing elite or an Establishment elite, the result is exactly the same. There are no real absolutes controlling either. In both cases one is left with only arbitrary absolutes set by a totalitarian society or state with all the modern means of manipulation under its control. Both the Left Wing elite and the rising Establishment elite are a threat.[32]

Like the animals in Orwell's *Animal Farm,* multiculturalists wind up looking and acting like the oppressors they seek to overthrow. Where there is no shared moral vision, public policies will be decided by who has the most power. There is nothing and no one else to appeal to.

Morality: from the Heart

Power imposed from outside is a sadly inadequate base for morality. Then where do morals reside? Early in his ministry, Jesus had this to say:

The good person out of the good treasure of the heart produces good, and the evil person out of evil treasure produces evil; for it is out of the abundance of the heart that the mouth speaks. (Lk 6:45 NRSV)

From a nonbeliever's perspective, Christian morals look like laws imposed from the outside by a church or some other religious authority. From the inside, where we live with ourselves every day, Christians know

that a person's actions—whether good or bad—reflect what is in the heart.
To understand the moral fervor of Christians, non-Christians must understand that our morality begins not with a list of commandments but with relationship. As a result of putting faith in Christ and knowing him, of course we try to follow him in our actions. His laws help us follow faithfully and more intelligently. They give us an objective reference when we're assaulted by doubts or pulled away by wishful thinking. Since we won't always feel like following God, his moral rules keep us from living by the whims of our feelings.

We know that God's laws are good, and we also know that our personal connection with the living God can never be established or maintained by law. Christians have always struggled with the tension between approaching life too legally and approaching it too mercifully. It's a good struggle, probably necessary for our spiritual health, but it is not often understood by outsiders.

Believe it or not, Christians really do fear legalism. "Do not judge," Jesus warned us, "or you too will be judged" (Mt 7:1). We are haunted by the recurring stories in the Gospels of how Jesus clashed with the Pharisees, who elevated law over vital relationship with God. We remember how he told them things like, "You blind guides! You strain out a gnat but swallow a camel" (Mt 23:24). In our best moments we fear the temptation to be self-righteous, to dot the i's and cross the t's but miss the merciful spirit of God's Word.

At the same time, we who know God's mercy also know his holiness, which makes that mercy necessary. Jesus made no apologies for harshly rebuking sin, such as in the two quotes above. No matter how much we would like to excuse a sinning person or ourselves, God's moral law still stands, and we do ourselves and others no favor by glossing over sin.

For example, along with Chancellor Joseph Fernandez, Christians agree that teen sex is a matter of life and death. We also believe there are many kinds of life and death—physical, emotional and spiritual. Teen sex is a moral issue because within each eager young body is an eternal soul. Teens' sexuality involves their relationships with one other as fellow humans; it also involves the moral responsibility of adults to be honest about the emotional and spiritual connections which are inseparably bound up with sexuality. Ultimately, we believe, the issue involves teens' relationship with their Creator, who made them sexual beings and who cares for every aspect of their personalities as well as their bodies.

Speaking Out Reluctantly

Though all Christians believe that morals begin in the heart, some feel called to fight the culture wars publicly by working to elect candidates and pass laws promoting Christian morality. Their activism in the past several elections has left two inaccurate impressions: that Christians are eager to dive into the political arena, and that when they dive they always come up on the conservative side.

Bible-believing Christians in the U.S. are mostly "conservative" (traditional) in morals, but in politics they range all over the continuum—left, right, center and floating. Christians' attitudes about politics should not be judged by which end of the spectrum is most vocal. "The religious right" (a phrase invented by its antagonists) speaks for some Christians but by no means all and probably not even most.

Despite the never-quit activism of the Christian Coalition, the average Christian hesitates to translate his or her personal faith into political action. Some don't see how faith can mix with the dirty world of politics. Some doubt there can be one "Christian" view on any issue. Some shun politics because they believe so strongly that people's hearts must change first, a change which can't be accomplished by political influence.

When Bill Jack was a high-school English teacher, it took one of his own students to motivate him to take the risk of bringing his faith to school. He described himself as "a compartmentalized Christian for the first five years of my teaching career."

I loved the Lord and worked with our church youth, but I'd swallowed the idea that faith had no place in the public classroom. Even in my literature classes I never mentioned the most influential work in Western civilization—the Bible. . . . I did nothing but wring my hands and bemoan the sad state of affairs.

Then one of my journalism students asked me to accompany him to the principal's office while he presented his case for the right to distribute Christian materials. That started me thinking. Of course the First Amendment's freedom of speech, press and assembly extends to believers too![33]

Most Christians who speak out on public policy do so reluctantly and only after a lot of soul-searching and prayer. We know that if we merely keep matching the other side push for shove, we will spend decades caught up in a strictly human and futile power struggle.

Gladly Pleading Guilty

There are times when as Christians we gladly plead guilty to pushing our morality on others. We believe that Christian morals, not left in the abstract but put into practice, have accomplished a great deal of good.

It was largely the influence of Christians like William Wilberforce that brought an end to the slave trade in the eighteenth century. Martin Luther King Jr.'s Southern Christian Leadership Conference mobilized for civil rights when few others in the country were speaking out; tributes to King today routinely overlook the fact that he was an ordained minister. Christians have led or joined the fight against abuses of all kinds, especially on behalf of those unable to defend themselves. Because we look to a higher authority for our moral guidance, we do not always choose the socially popular causes.

Certainly Christians have often been guilty of supplementing God's moral code with our own trivial additions. But can anyone come up with a better moral code than what we find in the basic teachings of the Bible?

The first four of the Ten Commandments given to Moses (Ex 20:1-17) refer to humanity's relationship with God. They tell us to accept our place as creations of God. We must not imagine that we ourselves are God, and we must not make our own gods to manipulate for our own purposes.

The concluding six commandments concern our relationships with each other. Consider a society in which children respect their parents, not as little robots but as willing learners who listen to their parents and see them as real people. Consider a society in which marriage partners love each other and stay faithful to each other sexually and in every other way.

Consider a society without theft or murder. Consider a society where you can trust others and they know they can trust you. Consider a society not driven by greed, at peace with itself because its people are satisfied.

Jesus was once asked which of God's commandments was most important. He did not choose one of the Ten but quoted two other passages in the Hebrew Scriptures which express the spirit of the Ten: "Love the Lord your God with all your heart and with all your soul and with all your mind and with all your strength" and "Love your neighbor as yourself" (Mk 12:30-31, quoting Deut 6:5 and Lev 19:18). Who would object to living in a society that looked and acted like that?

The Uniqueness of Christianity
Even if we demonstrate what's good about Christian morality, there is still an unanswered question: What's *Christian* about Christian morality? Can't all religions claim the same morality? The Ten Commandments and the verses Jesus quoted to sum up God's Law aren't even from the New Testament; they belong to the Hebrew Scriptures. Other religions teach love, respect, faithfulness, devotion to God, self-control. Couldn't even atheists live by the same good moral rules that Christians do?

The uniqueness of Christianity is what can happen between God and a person when that person does *not* live by the good moral rules, but fails miserably and rebels against God. The uniqueness of Christianity is the offer of forgiveness bought by Christ himself—paid for by his death—to which a person of faith responds not by harder effort but by simply accepting Christ's mercy.

One of Jesus' disciples, John, wrote in his later years about two possible attitudes toward sin:

> If we claim to be without sin, we deceive ourselves and the truth is not in us. If we confess our sins, he is faithful and just and will forgive us our sins and purify us from all unrighteousness. (1 Jn 1:8-9)

For those who accept Christ's forgiveness, Christianity offers the promise of inner moral renewing through the Holy Spirit. Not long before he died, knowing his time was short, Jesus promised his followers the resource of his Spirit living in them, helping them to live his way:

If you love me, you will obey what I command. And I will ask the Father, and he will give you another Counselor to be with you forever—the Spirit of truth. The world cannot accept him, because it neither sees him nor knows him. But you know him, for he lives with you and will be in you. I will not leave you as orphans; I will come to you. (Jn 14:15-18)

When we claim "I'm a Christian," we don't mean first of all that we follow a roster of Jesus' marching orders. We mean that we have come into a new relationship with God by accepting his forgiveness (secured by Christ's death) for not following his commandments. Our lifelong prayer and aim is then that we will draw on his power to become more like him in our character, "being transformed," as Paul wrote, "into his likeness with ever-increasing glory, which comes from the Lord, who is the Spirit" (2 Cor 3:18).

A Matter of Heart

Do Christians think there's any moral hope for our society? Most of us waver between pessimism and optimism. In his book *Generation at Risk*, Fran Sciacca names four moral stages which U.S. society has passed through: "Biblical Morality," "Abiblical Morality," "Immorality" and "Amorality."[34] The pattern belongs not only to U.S. history but to the history of God's people in the Bible.

One generation will be energized with spiritual renewal, come to God and try to live by his standards because they love and trust him. The next generation will be raised with godly morals and will follow them but won't have a grasp of why, other than "this is how I was raised." The next generation will rebel against the outdated morals and throw them away because there is no reason to keep them. The following generation will drift in the vacuum of amorality, having not even the memory of any moral standards. Out of people's desperate need another spiritual revival will come.

At all those societal stages there are still individual people whose religion is sincere and lively and whose morals are not masks but come from the heart. A vital teaching of both Jewish and Christian faith is that

God keeps a "remnant" of faithful people alive, witnessing to his holiness and his mercy. From the witness and prayers of the remnant, by God's mercy, spiritual renewal comes again. People turn back to God. Their behavior changes because they are changed inside by the Holy Spirit. Morals are internalized, and society is renewed because people are renewed. This is the "revival" that Christians hope and pray for—first spiritual, then inevitably moral.

2/ "Christianity Suppresses Women"

MYTH #2: "The church through the ages has stifled the voices and gifts of women and has treated women as second-class beings."

Get thee to a nunnery. Go, farewell.
—Hamlet spurning Ophelia (Act III, Scene 1)

For some time in another city we belonged to a church whose governing council was the board of deacons. Following the convictions of this church and the pattern in the book of Acts, the deacon board was always made up of seven men. There was also a group of women called deaconesses who were chosen to help with various needs at the request of the deacon board or pastor.

While we deaconesses met monthly for prayer, over the course of a year or so we were given little else to do. Finally at one deaconess meeting, one of the women (not this author) suddenly expressed her frustration: "What's our purpose, anyway? Why isn't the church doing anything with us? Why aren't we being called on more often to serve?" It came out that all of us were feeling the same way.

The deaconesses set up a meeting with the deacons to explain our confusion over our purpose and to ask for clearer direction. The deacons responded good-naturedly. They said they weren't sure either why the church had deaconesses, and maybe on down the line the church should take another look at that, but for now it might be best if the deaconesses disbanded.

It was with a mingled sigh of relief and huff of frustration that we quit being deaconesses. More interesting is what happened next. The end of the official role of deaconess was hardly the end of ministry for any of those women, either in the church or outside it. We all had our involvements with people and we would maintain them, and we all found various ways to serve both in and outside the church.

That encounter between deaconesses and deacons reenacted in miniature what has long happened with women seeking meaningful ministry within the church. Women desire a certain opening for service. It is denied by men. The women are miffed, but then they go elsewhere and find other, perhaps more meaningful ministry—with or without a lingering bad taste in the mouth.

Mostly Men Up Front

The question of women's place in the Christian church is as old as the church. Not that there was ever any doubt that women and men have equal access to the grace of God in Christ—but there were practical questions about how Christian men and women should relate to one another.

Male leadership, even dominance, has long been a "given" in the Christian church, and in much of the church it still is assumed. Walk into any Catholic or white evangelical Protestant church in the U.S. and you are likely to see a man standing behind the pulpit. Even if there is no pulpit and the front of the church is a stage with drum sets, electronic keyboard and colored lights, there's likely to be a woman in a prominent place only if she's singing a solo.

The rarity of women up front in church is no statistical coincidence. It reflects many mixed influences, both sincere and selfish.

One chapter of one book cannot possibly do justice to the subject of women and the church. We can only concentrate on the most persistent charges which get thrown in the face of Christianity. In the process we hope to bring to light some obscure and surprising facts which will put a new spin on the issues.

Dangerous Females

Controversy about women's place rose early in the church's history. For example, there are a number of surviving messages by John Chrysostom (Bishop of Constantinople A.D. 398-404) concerning the Scriptures and the proper conduct of the Christian life. In his *Homily 9 on 1 Timothy,* Chrysostom comments on the apostle Paul's prohibition on women teaching men. Paul's grounds were that the first woman, Eve, was deceived, became a sinner and led Adam into sin. (More later about that passage and Paul's views.) Here is how Chrysostom interpreted Paul's prohibition:

> The woman taught once and for all, and upset everything. Therefore he says, "Let her not teach." Then does it mean something for the rest of womankind, that Eve suffered this judgment? It certainly does concern other women! For the female sex is weak and vain, and here this is said of the whole sex.[1]

Medieval Catholicism, though it venerated Mary the mother of Jesus, was still prone to find perverseness in women.

> The belief that women practiced spells and cohabited with demons—acts that were viewed as solid evidence of their being witches—made them the brunt of vicious accusations that often resulted in trials and executions. Women were many times more likely to be executed for witchcraft than were men. . . . Indeed, the witchcraft frenzy of the late Middle Ages was one of the most sexist atrocities to have occurred in all of history.[2]

Historian Vern Bullough comments, "Sometimes it almost seems as if the church fathers felt that woman's only purpose was to tempt man from following the true path of righteousness."[3] Even after the Protestant Reformation, women in Europe were spiritually suspect. Good women were prone to be deceived by false doctrines, and bad ones were temptresses who led good men astray.

What is significant about the Protestant Reformation in regard to women is that while there was a change in viewpoint toward women as wives and their worth as human beings, the theological perspective on their role in the church had changed very little from the perspective that pervaded the medieval Catholic church. The concept of the priesthood of believers . . . did not open the door for equality of men and women in the church. Women were excluded from leadership positions and office holding.[4]

While there were outstanding exceptions, a negative image of women persisted when the Protestant church spread to the New World.

In the early decades of the colonial settlements (1630s to 1650s) the ancient image of "the bad woman" so prominent in medieval thought and witchcraft lingered on, especially in New England. The minds of women were thought to be incapable of handling anything more than basic learning. . . . Learning for women was not only inappropriate and futile, but also dangerous. Governor John Winthrop was convinced that the wife of Mr. John Hopkins of Connecticut had lost her sanity "by occasion of her giving herself wholly to reading and writing" and by meddling in things proper to men.[5]

A Worldwide Pattern

The story of women in the church has its grim aspects, but we need to remember it is only one segment of the story of women throughout time. By any account, regardless of the prevailing culture or religion, women's road through history has been rocky. Male dominance has been generally true in cultures worldwide. For example, legal documents of the ancient Middle East tell the story of the social place (or non-place) of women:

Women basically were property. They were neither to be seen nor heard. Monogamy was the normal way of life but monogamy in practice meant something different for the man than for the woman. A wife who slept with another man was an adulteress, but a man could not only visit prostitutes but in practice also took secondary wives as concubines. Rich men and royalty often had more than one legal wife. Women were always under the control of a male. Until the time her of marriage a girl remained under the protection of her father, who was free to settle her in marriage exactly as he thought fit. Once married she was under the control of her husband.[6]

The religion of Islam, coming in the seventh century A.D., introduced some reforms but continued to give religious justification for the subjugation of women, because "on earth, where God had made man superior to woman, women were to be subject to their nearest male relative, whose right over them was similar to his right over any of his other property."[7]

During the same time period in Europe, "polygamy was common among most of the Germanic tribes. Wives were bought and sold; rape was treated as theft; and husbands could repudiate wives with little ceremony."[8] As the influence of Roman and Christian law gained effect, wives were given more protection and rights, including the inheritance of property. "At least by the tenth century, Anglo-Saxon women had considerable power over property."[9] Still the males dominated.

[T]he record of women through the medieval millennium . . . can be charted as a series of advances and retreats: relatively high in Romanized Europe at the end of the Empire; relatively low in the early centuries of the barbarian kingdoms; advancing with the civilizing influence of Christianity and contact with Roman culture; cresting at the end of the Dark Ages when women assumed economic and legal responsibilities to free men for military action; leveling off or possibly declining under the new restrictions of feudalism, which yet permitted women to act as regents, command castles, work side by side with men in the fields and city shops, and form the main audience for the new romantic poetry, basis for the future salon; finally, at the end of the Middle Ages, turning downward as bureaucratized government and commercial capitalism eroded women's role in politics and the economy.[10]

So goes much of women's history in this flawed world. And we need to remember that the Christian church exists in this flawed world, not somewhere miles above the surface of society. The church consists of fallen human beings. We have admitted our rebellion against God and have accepted his forgiveness, and the life of Christ is remaking us. Even today, in various ways, including power struggles between males and females, the church often participates in the world's prevailing values.

Signs of Change

Has there been progress for women in the Christian church? Yes. How do we measure it? That gets more difficult. The yardstick which immediately comes to many minds is ordination to the pastorate—that is, whether women can fully serve as professionals in the ministry. When we use that measuring rod we see positive signs of progress for women. According to a 1997 report on seminary enrollment:

> In the 1976-77 school year, only about 12 percent of entering students nationwide were female. By the 1986-87 school year, that figure jumped to nearly 22 percent. This trend shows no sign of changing. One school reported an entering class with a little over 29 percent women for the 1996-97 school year. . . . [M]ore women than ever are seeking theological training, and more will be attracted to seminary to equip themselves for the increasing opportunities coming their way.[11]

Today if we walk into a mainline Protestant church ("mainline" meaning one of the old denominations well established in America since Colonial times), there is some possibility that the robed minister up front will be a woman. In some mainline denominations, such as the Methodist church, the tradition of women exercising leadership goes far back in history.

Too Big for the Kitchen

In the winter of 1711-12 Susanna Wesley, in the absence of her Anglican minister husband Samuel, began expounding on the Scriptures in her home on Sunday evenings. At first she taught only her own family and some neighbors, but other people soon joined the gatherings. "As the crowds became too big for her kitchen, the two hundred people spread throughout the whole house and barn."[12]

Among Samuel and Susanna Wesley's nineteen children growing up in this atmosphere were John, founder of the Methodist movement, and Charles, author of thousands of Christian hymns sung today in churches of all denominations. The spiritual revival which the Wesley brothers led in England and the First Great Awakening in America "changed people's attitudes about women proclaiming the good news. Through the revivals, women were given the place that the Reformation had failed to give them."[13]

In such a climate, it was easy for John Wesley to follow his mother's teaching and appoint women as local preachers and itinerant ministers. At first he did so cautiously by suggesting that women give five-minute expositions on Scripture. But then a crisis arose. His leading evangelist died suddenly, and the evangelist's wife, Sarah Millett, was taking care of his parish. In fact, she was preaching to crowds as large as two or three thousand people. . . . When in 1787, ten years later, the issue was raised about whether or not Sarah Millett should be officially recognized as a Methodist minister, what could John Wesley do but give her the right hand of fellowship?[14]

Who Has Muzzled Whom?

The stereotype persists that liberal activist churches have given women freedom while conservative churches have muzzled women. Historically this is not the way things happened. The mainline denominations in America still ordain relatively few women ministers, and those who are ordained often have a hard time finding churches willing to employ them as pastors. Meanwhile certain evangelical groups which left (or were forced out of) mainline churches began very early to recognize women and men as equals in ministry.

It is an important fact of history that the institutionalized churches most strongly opposed women in ministry. This is particularly evident in the Protestant churches in America. While the sectarian movements often encouraged active women's involvement, the mainline denominations resisted it.[15]

Sometimes a new evangelical movement gave women freedom in the first rush of revival and growth. As the movement consolidated its strength and firmed up into an institution, power struggles rose and doors were closed to women—doors which have only recently begun to re-open.

My Best Men Are Women

In certain evangelical groups, such as the Salvation Army, women have consistently enjoyed freedom to minister and have had great effect, to the point of becoming legendary. While the secular world notices the

Salvation Army mainly at Christmas and at times of natural disaster, it is a strong and active church in its own right. It was co-founded by the husband-and-wife team of William and Catherine Booth.

While William Booth was still a Methodist minister, his wife Catherine obeyed an inner prompting and stood up to speak in a packed church service. "William apparently was not threatened by the potential competition of her ministry. Soon after her pulpit debut, William became ill, and his slow recovery opened the door for her own preaching ministry."[16] In 1865 the Booths, having broken with Methodism, began a mission in West London which was the root of the Salvation Army. In the Army's 1875 "Foundation Deed," clause 14 guaranteed women's rights to participate fully in all aspects of the mission's work.

From the very beginning, the Salvation Army welcomed the service of women. . . . In 1878, only three years after clause 14 was formulated, forty-one of the total ninety-one Salvation Army officers in the field were women.[17]

So important were women workers to the mission of the Salvation Army that William Booth ventured to say, "My best men are women."[18]

And They Will Prophesy

At the first Pentecost, after Jesus' resurrection, the Holy Spirit suddenly came on the apostles and they began proclaiming the gospel in languages they didn't even know, so the foreigners around them understood the message. The apostle Peter explained what was happening by quoting the prophet Joel:

In the last days, God says,
I will pour out my Spirit on all people.
Your sons and daughters will prophesy,
your young men will see visions,
your old men will dream dreams.
Even on my servants, both men and women,
I will pour out my Spirit in those days,
and they will prophesy.
(Acts 2:17-18)

Joel's prophecy, fulfilled at Pentecost, is taken by Pentecostal believers and most in the newer charismatic movement to mean that all believers can be used by God to proclaim his Word. Therefore all Christians, regardless of gender or age, have freedom to speak out in an assembly of believers and say what they believe the Holy Spirit is saying.

Called and Gifted

The Free Methodist Church originated in the U.S. around the time of the Civil War when certain Methodist clergy took a stand against slavery and were asked to leave the church. In tune with his stance for equality of all people, founder B. T. Roberts supported the ordination of any person whom God had called to preach, regardless of race or gender. In his book *Ordaining Women* he wrote:

> The Gospel of Jesus Christ . . . knows no distinction of race, condition, or sex, therefore no person evidently called of God to the Gospel ministry, and duly qualified for it, should be refused ordination on account of race, condition or sex.[19]

A person "evidently called of God" and "duly qualified"—those are the crucial tests.

For B. T. Roberts, for John Wesley a century earlier, and for others who came around to the view that women could preach and teach, the deciding factor was not that women demanded a voice or influence in the church. The test was the evidence of the Holy Spirit's power working through the people God had chosen. If there was evidence that God had chosen a person to proclaim his message, how could a church deny that person a voice?

Beyond Ordination

Being granted a voice in ministry may or may not mean formal ordination. Different churches interpret "ordination" in different ways. Churches validate God's call to ministry—for both males and females—in various forms. Some grant women ordination to the pastorate, some a license to preach, some a license as a lay minister or some other recognition of gifts and call. If we judge the extent of women's participation in church ministry solely by the issue of ordination to the pastorate, we restrict the amazing diversity of women's influence in the church.

Women have exerted great influence in many areas of church life simply because men were not interested in those areas and left them to the ladies. Many women have been delighted to move into those areas, where they can minister freely. They chafe at current attempts to absorb "women's ministries" into (for example) more inclusive Christian Education committees, often headed by men. The women's ministries have been functioning freely for years with their own budgets, agendas and organizational structure. They would prefer to remain separate and independent, unconcerned about where they fit in any church hierarchy.

When Sunday School Was School
Sunday school, now typically a tame and orderly hour just before worship, began in England as a social rescue effort for children who labored in factories Monday through Saturday. The Sunday school was literally a school where factory children had their only opportunity for basic education. "[W]ithout women, the movement would never have flourished. Robert Raikes, considered the founder of the Sunday-school movement, began his work in the 1780s with four women, who held weekly Bible classes for children."[20]

To this day women carry the major load of Sunday-school teaching, at least of students younger than college age. Anyone who thinks Sunday-school teaching is a trivial or inconsequential role should know that it is very typical for a Christian man in a leadership position to credit the life-changing influence of a female Sunday-school teacher.

Henrietta Mears became director of Christian education at the First Presbyterian Church of Hollywood, California, in 1928. Though she staunchly believed that women should not preach, and she did not teach males older than college age, she revolutionized Christian education in America. Gospel Light publishing company rose from Mears's efforts and continues as a major publisher today. Evangelist Billy Graham, Campus Crusade for Christ founder Bill Bright and former U.S. Senate chaplain Richard Halverson as young men were all deeply influenced by Mears.[21]

Mears was driven by her conviction that she was training the next generation of world leaders. And almost incidentally, in the course of so doing, she raised the concept of Sunday school to new levels. "Don't ever say 'I'm just a Sunday-school teacher,'" she used to say. "You are a teacher in Christ's college. Be proud that you teach!"[22]

Women on the Mission Field

Finding the doors of many traditional missionary societies closed to single females, women in the nineteenth century began their own societies to send out women missionaries.

Although a few single women did receive sponsorship from established mission boards in the early decades of the nineteenth century, the discrimination they faced created a new concept of foreign missionary support—the "female agency." . . . By 1900 there were more than forty women's mission societies in the United States alone. Largely because of the "female agencies," the number of single women in missions rapidly increased, and during the first decade of the twentieth century women, for the first time in history, outnumbered men in Protestant missions—in some areas by large proportions.[23]

In many remote areas of the "uncivilized" world, single women proved more effective than male missionaries. They were less threatening to the native people, and they often had more staying power. Men were less willing to go to the ends of the earth single, and married men faced the unavoidable distractions of family life. While many missionary wives felt called by God to serve overseas, others accompanied their husbands half-willingly, afraid for their children's welfare—with good reason, as many missionaries watched their children die in infancy. The single woman missionary faced loneliness and danger, but she was free of the cares of family.

Single women have been among the pioneers in the modern missionary movement. As early as 1882, missionary societies started for women had sent out and supported 694 unmarried women in world mission. The same year, the China Inland Mission had 56 wives and 95 single women in China. And already in 1888, Hudson Taylor, the founder of the C.I.M., reported many stations in inland China were being "manned" by single women. By 1900, according to R. Pierce Beaver, dean of American missiologists, there were 1,015 single women missionaries sent out from the United States. This number more than doubled to 2,122 in 1910, and redoubled to 4,824 in 1923.[24]

The single woman missionary also had open doors for ministry which were closed to her at home. "Foreign missions attracted women for a variety of reasons, but one of the most obvious was that there were few opportunities for women to be involved in a full-time ministry in the homeland. Christian service was considered a male profession."[25] This led to strange paradoxes, such as Florence Young of the Plymouth Brethren preaching the gospel and teaching male converts in the islands of the South Pacific, while she would not have been allowed to do either in her assembly back home in Sydney, Australia.

Even in the most restrictive churches, the words of women regularly praise God and encourage and instruct the people. Flip through any hymnbook and note the writers of the hymn *words*. Often they are women, not only in newer hymnals whose editors have made the effort to include female writers, but also in older hymnals. Through the texts of their hymns these women speak freely to and for the church.

What It Was Meant to Be

It's futile to look for one monolithic Christian view of where women fit in church life. Various branches of Christianity have various interpretations, and all support them scripturally. Most enjoy fellowship with each other and respect each other's right to varying convictions, though privately they may grumble about each other.

But no number of examples of women functioning effectively in Christian ministry can disguise the fact that putdowns of women have happened and do happen in all branches of the church. Power plays happen in the church as in any organization which involves humans.

To be thoroughly fair to Christianity, we must look at the Bible—at what this faith is meant to be, not how it has been perverted or misused. We can start at the beginning. The book of Genesis gives two accounts of the creation of woman. The first says, "So God created humankind in his image, in the image of God he created them; male and female he created them" (1:27 NRSV). In the second, more detailed account, Adam is formed first. When no "suitable helper" is found for Adam, God puts him into a deep sleep, opens his side, takes one of his ribs and forms a woman. God brings her to the man, who is delighted (2:7, 20-23).

Throughout the Old Testament, women are mostly in a role subservient to and dependent on men—a situation typical of pastoral or farming societies. The husband and the father negotiated a marriage contract that often included the exchange of property or service. Women were explicitly excluded from the Jewish priesthood.

On the other hand, there were special laws to provide for widows (Deut 14:28-29) and to limit a man's right to divorce his wife (Deut 24:1-4). Moses' sister Miriam is recognized as having a leadership role and being a prophetess in Exodus 15; she writes a song of victory over the Egyptians, and it is included in Scripture here. Deborah, Esther and Huldah are among the other women mentioned in the Old Testament as leaders or prophetesses. The ideal wife described in Proverbs 31 buys and sells merchandise and land, commands a number of servants and provides for her household.

Jesus and Women

One of the many times when Jesus was criticized by religious leaders because he associated with tax collectors and sinners, he responded by telling three parables (Lk 15). Each story illustrates in human terms how God himself actively seeks lost people.

In the first parable, God is a shepherd with 100 sheep. Unsatisfied that ninety-nine of them are safe, he goes out searching for the one lost sheep and joyfully carries it home on his shoulders. In the third and most famous parable, the story of the prodigal son, God is the faithful and forgiving father who sees his returning son at a distance and runs to welcome him back.

Tucked between those two touching parables is the story of the woman who loses one of her ten precious silver coins. She sweeps the house and searches for it, and when she finds it—like the shepherd and the father—

she stages a celebration. Overturning cultural expectations, Jesus had no reservations about using the searching woman, just as he used the diligent shepherd and the waiting father, to illustrate the heart of God.

As an example of generosity, Jesus pointed out a poor woman who put the last of her money into the temple treasury; he said she had given more than all the rich people (Mk 12:41-44). As an example of persistent prayer, Jesus told a parable about a woman who kept pleading with an unjust judge (Lk 18:1-8). He used ten female virgins with lamps to illustrate the need for all Christians, male and female, to be always ready for his return (Mt 25:1-13).

In the village of Bethany near Jerusalem, Jesus was a guest at the home of the sisters Martha and Mary and their brother Lazarus, whom he would later raise from the dead. Martha got busy with lots of preparations, but Mary "sat at the Lord's feet listening to what he said." When Martha complained, Jesus defended Mary (Lk 10:38-42). Here was Martha in the traditional role of the woman, busy in the kitchen, working to meet the needs of her household and guests. Jesus was not defending Mary's idleness but rather her right to learn from him. Sitting at the teacher's feet was the typical posture of the student or disciple. The apostle Paul spoke of himself as "brought up in this city at the feet of Gamaliel" his rabbinic teacher (Acts 22:3 KJV). To sit at the feet of the master was not wasting time or indulging one's curiosity; it was preparing for future service.

Perhaps Jesus' most remarkable encounter with a woman is his conversation with the woman at Jacob's well, just outside the town of Sychar (Jn 4:1-42). She was a Samaritan—a member of the mixed Jewish-Gentile race whom Jews scorned. She was living an immoral life. Any Jewish male, especially a rabbi, would have considered her less than nothing. Yet Jesus risked his reputation by initiating a public conversation with her, and he put himself in the needy position by asking for a drink of water. She was one of the first people to whom he revealed his identity as the Christ (v. 26).

The woman left her water jar and headed into town to tell everyone she had found the Messiah. On the way she passed his disciples, who were coming back from town where they had gone to buy food. Jesus had neither gone into town himself nor sent his disciples there to preach. He simply taught a woman, won her to himself and left to her the job of spreading the good news.

In the accounts of Mary of Bethany and the woman at the well, we see the possibilities Jesus considered acceptable for women. When we look at Jesus' attitude toward women in a society which often ignored them, it is easy to see why women followed him, remained near the cross as he died and arrived first at the empty tomb.

First with the Message

We could even say that women became the first apostles, that is, the "ones sent" with the message of the risen Christ. All four Gospel writers affirm that women first discovered that Jesus had risen from the dead (Mt 28:1-10; Mk 16:1-8; Lk 24:1-12, 22-24; Jn 20:1-18). The Gospel writers did not have to credit these women. Certainly they did not have to identify any of them by name, but all four writers name at least one, and Mark and Luke name three.

Luke, the careful historian who picked and chose his details, left in one detail which to this day still hits the reader like a punch in the stomach. The women hurried from the empty tomb and told the apostles that Christ was risen, "but these words seemed to them an idle tale, and they did not believe them" (Lk 24:11 RSV). The church's Easter story includes the disbelief of the male apostles in the face of female testimony. Robert McAfee Brown says Luke's statement "only proves that within a few hours of its creation the Christian church was guilty of male chauvinism."[26] Such admission of disbelief should have been a deep embarrassment to the male-dominated church. Yet for two thousand years the church has openly admitted the doubt of the male disciples and the contrasting belief of the women.

Quotes That Can't Be Culled

The fiercest opponents of Christianity recognize the tender and accepting attitude of Jesus toward women. Even radical feminist theologians "believe that they can convert Christianity into the gender-free faith which they are certain Jesus intended."[27] It isn't Jesus but some of his followers past and present who are to be blamed for shutting women out of the church.

While the New Testament documents were still being written, questions came up about women's role in the church. So some details of the conflicts—and the apostolic responses—made it into the Scriptures. There they are today, all the difficult passages about wives submitting to their husbands, women being forbidden to teach or have authority over men, Eve (and by extension all women) being to blame for sin coming into the world. Lots of well-meaning people have tried to cull these embarrassments from the Bible. Except for some minor discrepancies in writing styles, however, there is no evidence that the sticky passages were inserted by woman-haters centuries after the original writings. It looks as if Paul and Peter really wrote those things.

Paul and Women: Down by the Riverside
The writings of the apostle Paul provide most of the biblical basis for male leadership and female subordination in church hierarchy. Paul is the biblical person targeted for the most blame for his negative attitude toward women. Well, why not? Paul wrote things like "Women should remain silent in the churches" (1 Cor 14:34), "Wives, submit to your husbands" (Eph 5:22) and "I do not permit a woman to teach or to have authority over a man" (1 Tim 2:12).

If we take Paul's statements in isolation and at face value, there is hardly reason to even discuss his attitude. We must either accept that this is what the Bible teaches and live with it, or else ignore it and deny the authority of the Bible. Those isolated statements, however, are not all the information we have about Paul's attitude toward women.

When Paul, Silas, Timothy and Luke were evangelizing the area which is now Turkey, Paul had a vision of a man in Macedonia (now Greece) pleading for him to come over and help. The missionaries traveled to the Roman colony of Philippi and on the Sabbath went outside the city gates to the river, expecting to find people at prayer. There they found a group of women. Their reaction was not to say "Well, there's nobody here but women; we might as well leave." Instead they sat down on the river bank and started talking with them. A wealthy woman named Lydia came to faith. Dorothy R. Pape, who as a Christian missionary in five different countries dealt with various cultural views of women, points out how Paul broke with tradition on the river bank:

> It was well that on this occasion Paul ignored the custom which dictated that a "good" man, and especially a rabbi, should not address a woman in public, for it was as a result of his speaking that Lydia believed, and one of the healthiest New Testament churches was formed in her home.[28]

Later in Corinth, Paul met a Jew named Aquila and his wife Priscilla and began to work with them both in evangelizing and in the trade of tentmaking. Paul traveled with the couple to Ephesus, where he left them to carry on the work. An eloquent but untrained Christian named Apollos arrived in Ephesus and began speaking in the local synagogue. The husband-and-wife team immediately saw that Apollos showed promise. "When Priscilla and Aquila heard him, they invited him to their home and explained to him the way of God more adequately" (Acts 18:26). Priscilla as well as Aquila is credited with instructing Apollos.

A Woman Deacon?

At the end of his letter to the church in Rome, Paul asks the Roman Christians to greet about twenty people, including Phoebe, who apparently carried his letter to them. Nearly half of those Paul mentioned are women, seven of whom he especially remembered. In Romans 16:1 Phoebe is called something which is variously translated "servant" (NIV and NASB), "deaconess" (RSV), "sister" (TEV), "leader" (CEV). In the original Greek the word is *diakonos,* the same word Paul used in 1 Timothy 3:8 concerning the church office of deacon. There is no feminine form of this word in Greek. It is used generally of servants and is also used of Christ and followers of Christ. The other word used to describe Phoebe is in the Greek *prostatis.* Romans 16:2 is the only place this word is used in the New Testament:

> "Helper" (NASB) or "help" (NIV) translates a Greek term applied especially to patrons. A patron of a religious association was normally a well-to-do person who allowed members of a religious group to meet

in his or her home. The patron was generally a prominent and honored member of the group and generally exercised some authority over it. Although most patrons of religious associations were men, some women patrons are known.[29]

In this same letter closing, Paul warmly speaks of Priscilla and Aquila equally as "fellow workers in Christ Jesus" who have "risked their lives" for him (Rom 16:3-4).

Paul and Marriage

Paul is often criticized as an ascetic foe of marriage, but when he writes about marriage in 1 Corinthians 7, he carefully describes a relationship of mutual submission.

> Each man should have his own wife, and each woman her own husband. The husband should fulfill his marital duty to his wife, and likewise the wife to her husband. The wife's body does not belong to her alone but also to her husband. In the same way, the husband's body does not belong to him alone but also to his wife. (vv. 2-4)

John Chrysostom "believed that the single sexual standard was the one point at which Christian wives enjoyed equality with their husbands."[30] He wrote in *Homily 19 on 1 Corinthians:*

> Therefore if you husbands ever spy a prostitute tempting you, say "My body is not mine, but my wife's." And the wife should likewise reply to those wishing to undermine her chastity, "My body is not mine, but my husband's."[31]

Paul "presupposes that mutual love and self-giving will be expressed in our sexuality. No ego-trip, no will to power, no seduction or rape is tolerated. Here is mutual surrender. Here is the meeting of each other's sexual needs and desires. . . . As Christ gave Himself for us, so we give ourselves for each other."[32]

Silent Women?

In his letter to the church at Corinth which we call 1 Corinthians, Paul takes on the need for proper order in Christian worship services, and he appears to reverse himself about the equality of men and women. It sounds as though he places the man in authority as the head of the woman, with Christ as the head of the man and God the head of Christ (11:3). He writes about the woman covering her head when she prays or prophesies, while the man should pray or prophesy with his head uncovered (11:4-10). Paul justifies his position because woman is the glory of man while man is the image and glory of God, the woman came from the man, and the woman was made for the man. "For this reason, and because of the angels, the woman ought to have a sign of authority on her head" (v. 10)—though Paul quickly assures his readers that in the Lord, men and women are not independent of each other (v. 11).

To Paul and his readers his meaning was no doubt clear, but how should we understand it today? In the whole discussion the only image familiar to our Western minds is that of the "head" being in authority. Most Bible commentators go on at great length explaining their positions on this difficult passage. Some have interpreted "head" as "source" rather than "authority," but in what sense are men the "source" of women? The debate has been heated and is still not resolved. We can say at least that if the passage is this obscure, it's not a passage on which to base a final decision about women's place in the church.

In 1 Corinthians 14, Paul continues his discussion of proper order in worship. After writing about speaking in tongues, interpretation of tongues and giving one another opportunity to speak, he says that "women should remain silent in the churches" (14:34).

His command creates a problem, because back in 11:5 Paul instructed women to cover their heads when they prophesy. Now a woman may be able to pray silently, but how can she prophesy silently? She cannot proclaim the word of God to others or foretell the future without speaking; yet doesn't Paul say "they are not allowed to speak" (14:34)? Some say Paul means women can prophesy only at all-woman gatherings. Others interpret his words to mean the women were chattering and discussing among themselves, distracting the men from worship. While there is no textual reason for the "chattering" interpretation, it does fit Paul's consistent emphasis on the need for order in worship.

No More Barriers

In his letter to the Galatians, Paul declared that in Christ the barriers between races, between social and economic classes, and between the two sexes are gone. His context is Christians' freedom from the Old Testament law and our new relationship as children of God in Christ (3:26-29). All of us who have been "baptized into Christ" have clothed ourselves with Christ. In the temple in Jerusalem there was an outer court of Gentiles, a court of women inside that, and then the inner court where Jewish males could gather and where sacrifices were made. Now Paul declares "there is neither Jew nor Greek, slave nor free, male nor female, for you are all one in Christ Jesus" (3:29).

Paul picks up the theme of unity in his letter to the Ephesians, and it's in this context that he gives the dreaded command "Wives, submit to your husbands as to the Lord" (Eph 5:22). In the original Greek, however, the word "submit" does not occur at all in verse 22. It does occur in verse 21: "Submit to one another out of reverence for Christ." Verse 22 is literally a continuation of the thought: "Wives in the same way to your husbands." Husbands are likewise told to "love your wives, just as Christ loved the church and gave himself up for her" (5:25).

In the New Testament period, there was nothing new in the idea of wives being submissive to their *husbands,* for, after all, that was a legal requirement; but it was a great departure from custom to request it voluntarily. What was utterly revolutionary, however, was the instruction to husbands. Both Peter and Paul have some amazing things to say about the *mutual* responsibilities of husband and wife.[33]

In 1 Timothy 2:9-15 Paul takes on the matters of women's appearance, quietness, submission and teaching. He seems to speak clearly about women not teaching or having authority over men, backing it up with Adam being formed first and Eve being the one who was deceived. But if Paul was referring to a woman usurping a man's place of authority, why does he use a Greek word for "authority" which is not used any other place in the New Testament? W. E. Vine defines the Greek verb as "to exercise authority on one's own account, to domineer over."[34] If women are being specifically told not to domineer, does Paul mean that men *should* domineer? Not likely.

Healthy Tension

How do we put all this data together? While Paul seems to make clear statements about women being silent in church and not teaching or having authority over men, he also commends several women for doing exactly those activities. While he seems to describe a hierarchy with Christ under the Father, the husband under Christ and the wife under the husband, he reminds the Christian husband that his body belongs not to himself but to his wife!

Jill Briscoe, author and wife of Stuart Briscoe, pastor of the huge Milwaukee-area Elmbrook Church, speaks of living with the healthy tension between her husband's leadership and husband-wife equality in Christ:

> I accept headship as a biblical concept. I also accept equality as another biblical concept. And just as I cannot bring predestination and free will together, I cannot bring headship and equality together, but I embrace them both.[35]

Service, Not Selfishness

It is unfair to leap to the conclusion that Christian men decide to take leadership solely through the desire to hold onto power; their leadership has also been the result of personal and theological conviction. It is also unfair to assume that all enlightened Christian women chafe under male leadership and covet leadership roles. There is the possibility that what seems oppressive to an outside observer may be comfortable and even liberating from the inside.

In a Christian community where a Christlike spirit reigns, men and women look for ways to serve each other, not rule over or manipulate each other. In a healthy church men and women get along, find their callings and yield to one another—because in a healthy church power is not the issue; service is the issue.

Not Because Society Says So

To serve Christ in a biblical sense, women as well as men must serve because they see needs and sense God's call—never because they crave power or even because they feel qualified and competent. If a woman or a man is demanding or craving ordination because it appears to be the most powerful position in the church, that isn't a Christlike mentality, it's a corporate mentality. There is always spiritual danger in focusing on something we feel capable of doing and insisting on doing it.

In the Bible, when God called men and women to a great task, they didn't respond, "Well, it's about time You noticed my abilities—I wondered when You'd get around to calling on me!" That's because God has always seen in men and women a potential that goes way beyond what they see in themselves.[36]

The Evangelical Covenant Church, descended from the Lutheran church in Scandinavia, has officially favored women's ordination only since 1976. The Board of Ministry makes the point that trends in secular society have no place in Christians' decisions about the course the church should take. The church looks elsewhere for its guidance:

The changes affecting women in the modern era have obviously influenced the Church's thinking, but the ministry of women is neither derived from society's ideas nor a partner to its extremes. For a tradition that is based on the question "Where is it written?" only one foundation is satisfactory for having women minister in the name of Jesus Christ. Women ought to minister not because society says so but because the Bible leads the Church to such a conclusion.[37]

Here is where Christian women and men have to turn to find the answers for where women and men belong in Christ's church. Our guidance comes neither from rigid tradition nor from popular whim, but from Christ.

3/ "Christianity Caused the Ecological Crisis"

MYTH #3: "The Christian religion is alienated from the natural world. The Bible says to subdue the earth, and Western Christian culture took that as a license to exploit nature."

The year's at the spring
And day's at the morn;
Morning's at seven;
The hill-side's dew-pearled;
The lark's on the wing;
The snail's on the thorn:
God's in his heaven—
All's right with the world!
—Robert Browning in "Pippa Passes"

Recently we moved to a medium-sized city after fifteen years in a small town. The home we bought here belonged to two sisters who had lived in it all their long lives. The neighbors tell us the women lived as though they were destitute—but after they died, money was found hidden everywhere in the house. (We keep looking but haven't located any more of the stash, so thanks for buying this book.)

Except for an old cast-iron sink, the kitchen was bare—not even any cabinets. A big drawback for selling the house, so the seller included a generous "appliance allowance" for the buyer. In twenty-five years of marriage we had hardly bought a new anything, let alone major appliances. Now we could even afford a few frills. In the Sears showroom the young salesman, a guy destined to go far in his profession, kept saying things like, "Now that's a fine refrigerator, but for only $49 more you can have . . ." It was intoxicating.

Like Woody the Woodpecker

Our new stove arrived a few days after we moved in; our refrigerator, on back order, arrived some time later. The stove fit right into its space, but in our small kitchen the refrigerator shocked us with its hugeness. It's nice, but do we need it? Of course not. We could have gotten by for a long time with the small loaner they gave us while the new refrigerator was on back order. But there the hulk sits, humming away, now and then making a tap-tap-tap noise as if Woody the woodpecker is living in the freezer.

Have Christians been guilty of overconsuming and wasting earth's resources? Of course some have, and some still do. Many Christians don't mean to misuse the earth but waste resources through carelessness.

Walk into the home of any Christian family and it's possible you'll find wasted food in the garbage or a faucet left running. They may use throwaway paper plates for no good reason, toss out aluminum foil just because it's wrinkled or drive a gas-hog car (or two or three). Some Christians even use their beliefs as an excuse for their careless attitude.

Golden Fleece, a self-sustaining farming and handcraft community in northern Wisconsin, was having a sort of mini-expo to display their techniques. As Dale wandered from sheep pen to garden plot, he struck up a conversation with another Christian, a man who was selling shares in a large communal garden. Naturally Dale brought up the question of what the Bible has to say about ecology and taking care of the earth. "Ecology?" the other man scoffed. "Why bother? It's all going to get burned up anyway."

Lumber, Furs and Gold

The man at Golden Fleece was acting out what many people assume is the Christian attitude toward this world. Christians talk a lot about looking forward to the return of Christ, when God will bring this world to a fiery apocalypse—from which, of course, they will be safely delivered. Why should Christians care about pollution or the ozone layer or the greenhouse effect when their time on earth is short and they're going to spend eternity breathing the pure air of heaven?

By contrast, the ancient earth religions seem to offer more hope for saving the planet. When those old religions reigned, the story goes, human beings knew their place as part of the whole. Before they cut down a tree or killed an animal, they said prayers to the guardian spirits, and they took from the land only as much as they needed to survive. All was in harmony between humanity and the rest of nature. But then the Europeans arrived, colonizing and infecting the Americas, Africa, Australia and just about everywhere else with the ideas of Western civilization.

Since Christianity was the dominant worldview in Europe for over a thousand years, particularly during the time of worldwide expansion and imperialism, then Europeans' arrogant assumptions about themselves and their place in the world must have come straight out of Christianity. In European religious artwork God is aloof, authoritarian, patriarchal, seated on a throne high among the stars with the earth beneath his feet. Church steeples pointed up away from the ground and toward the distant sky. When the Christian invaders looked at new lands, they did not see sacred forests or mountains where spirits lived; they saw lumber, furs and gold.

Humanity's Job Description

Critics who say Christianity is anti-nature like to point out that at the very beginning of the Bible, in the book of Genesis, God commanded humanity to subdue the earth and have dominion over every living creature. The commands were given immediately after God made people in his own image:

> And God blessed them, and God said unto them, Be fruitful, and multiply, and replenish the earth, and subdue it: and have dominion over the fish of the sea, and over the fowl of the air, and over every living thing that moveth upon the earth. (Gen 1:28 KJV)

That's how the passage goes in the King James Bible, still cherished by many Christians. A more modern translation, the New International Version, translates this verse

God blessed them and said to them, "Be fruitful and increase in number; fill the earth and subdue it. Rule over the fish of the sea and the birds of the air and over every living creature that moves on the ground."

In the Genesis version of creation, critics say, nature loses its sacred mystery and becomes an opponent for humanity to overcome, civilize and plunder. Christianity is meant to be an other-worldly religion. The great hope of Christians is not to save the earth for future generations but to leave this world and live "up there" with God.

The Historical Roots of the Accusation

While several writers have traced our environmental problems to the dominance of Christianity, the person who first popularized the blame was Lynn White Jr., in his 1967 *Science* magazine article "The Historical Roots of Our Ecologic Crisis."[1]

Dr. White's route to environmental renown was odd, since he was not an ecologist or even a scientist; he was a professor of medieval and Renaissance history who had written several books on the development of Western culture. His article happened to appear in a popular magazine precisely when two earthshaking changes were taking place in America: a mutiny against historic values on university campuses and in the streets, and the realization that we were running out of places to put all our trash.

Why, White asked, are we in imminent danger of destroying our own natural environment? Because our society holds certain unexamined assumptions about the world and our place in it.

We continue today to live, as we have lived for about 1700 years, very largely in a context of Christian axioms. . . . Our daily habits of action . . . are dominated by an *implicit faith in perpetual progress* which was unknown either to Greco-Roman antiquity or to the Orient. It is rooted in, and is indefensible apart from, Judeo-Christian teleology.[2]

In other words, Christians perceive human history not as a series of random events but as purposefully going somewhere. The Christian concept is in sharp contrast to the endless cycle of birth and death in Hindu thinking or the unpredictable antics of Greek and Roman gods.

The next logical assumption is that if history is going somewhere by God's plan, then life on earth is bound to get better. Change is good because it means old unprogressive ways are giving way to new improved methods. Propelled by the Christian outlook, the West developed an unquestioned faith in progress, which most people now realize is deadly for the health of the planet. It leads to unchecked economic growth and crowded cities and smoky industries and styrofoam fast-food containers and eight-lane highways and megamalls. Progress takes nature, stuffs it in a black plastic bag and dumps it in the landfill.

Another reason Christians do not respect nature, according to White, is that Christianity is "the most anthropocentric religion the world has seen." Christians see human beings as the highest point of creation because only human beings are made in the image of God. Instead of affirming that we are part of nature, Christianity sets up a fatal opposition between nature and humanity.

The gavel for the final verdict sounded when White declared that Christianity "not only established a dualism of man and nature but also insisted that it is God's will that man exploit nature for his proper ends."

Lynn White's article became a classic, and its powerful arguments became gospel for many environmentalists. Christians have spent the past three decades either answering or ignoring his accusations.

Christians Can Shut God Out
In the past few years several well-known Christian leaders have confessed to sexual immorality or financial misdealings. Despite what they said in public, privately they shut God out of certain areas of their lives. The results were devastating for those who fell and for those who trusted them.

The same tragedy happens when Christians exclude God (or think they can exclude God) from their dealings with the natural creation. The results are devastating for the earth and its creatures, including people. Unfortunately the church has always had a tendency to adopt the values of the surrounding culture, which in North America includes wastefulness of resources.

Sample Responses

Some Christians deny—often quite articulately—that there is any ecological crisis at all. They point out that God is the Sustainer of his creation as well as Creator, and God is not going to let his creation collapse.[3] Environmental "alarmists" are seen as mostly earth-worshipers using the environment as a screen for spreading New-Age goddess religion.[4]

Some Christians are unconcerned about scarcity because they sincerely believe that God will take care of them and will provide what they need. While their faith in God is genuine, it can also be short-sighted if they lack concern for the rest of the world, where it's less obvious that God is taking care of people.

Many Christians refuse to be alarmed about impending worldwide disaster, whether through bombs or the greenhouse effect. One Christian told us, "I'm not worried about nuclear war, because I know if it happens, I won't be here." She expects that Christ will take all Christians safely to heaven before the bombs fall.

Historically (we'll look at this more in the next chapter) many American church leaders have embraced the idea of guaranteed perpetual progress. Clergymen at the turn of the twentieth century allied themselves with big business and welcomed the prospects of an economic boom. A common theological view of the day was that humanity would keep improving until it ushered in a golden age, and then Christ would return.

Some Christians believe it's arrogant to think that we humans will have the final say about the fate of the earth. When the world comes to an end, it will be accomplished by God and not by human folly.

And yes, there are Christians, like the one we quoted, who believe that what happens to this earth is unimportant because it will all be burned up anyway.

Inherent in Christianity?

Christians have sometimes acted wrongly toward God's creation. But there is a vital difference between admitting that some Christians have failed to take care of the earth and asserting that there is something inherent in Christianity which is harmful to the environment.

We fully agree with Lynn White that "the roots of our trouble are largely religious." Environmental destruction comes when people express their ultimate values at nature's expense. There is, however, no historical foundation for singling out the Christian religion for promoting an exploitative view of nature.

Even White had to admit that ecological devastation is not unique to Western "Christian" cultures. The lower Nile River in pre-Christian times, he wrote, was "a human artifact rather than the swampy African jungle which nature, apart from man, would have made it." He also pointed out that North Africa used to be heavily forested before the Romans cut the trees to build ships, profoundly altering the ecology of that area.

In the 1950s, China was often cited as an example of what happens when a country fails to protect its soil from erosion. Chinese geographer Yi-fu Tuan confirms:

> Visitors to China in the nineteenth and early part of the twentieth centuries have often commented on the treelessness of the North, and the acute problems of soil erosion. . . . These areas were once well wooded. Deforestation on a vast scale took place as population increased and more and more land was taken over by farmers. . . . One [other factor] was the ancient custom, first recorded in the fourth century B.C., of burning trees in order to deprive dangerous animals of their hiding places. Even in contemporary China farmers are known to start fires for no evident purpose.
>
> Forests in North China were also depleted to make charcoal for industrial fuel. From the tenth century on, the expanding metallic industries swallowed up many hundreds of thousands of tons of charcoal each year, as did the manufacture of salt, alum, bricks, tile and liquor. By the Sung dynasty (A.D. 960-1279) the demand for wood and charcoal as both household and industrial fuels had exceeded the timber resources of the country; the result was the increasing substitution of coal for wood and charcoal.[5]

In North America, the Hudson Bay Company and the Northwest Company set up trading posts across the continent to trade with Native Americans for pelts to make fashionable beaver hats. During the seventeenth and eighteenth centuries, an army of voyageurs transported trade goods west and carried beaver pelts back to the East Coast for shipment to Europe. While whites provided the market, in the early days it was Native Americans who willingly provided the pelts in exchange for the white traders' trinkets, knives and blankets.

The evidence is that the history of disrespect for nature is much broader than Western culture with its Judeo-Christian heritage.

Harmony or Fear?

Animism is the technical name for the belief that there are unseen spirits in all things, not only animals and trees but even what Westerners would call inanimate things such as rocks. Animism is often romanticized as an awareness of the sacredness of nature. Because traditional indigenous peoples are typically animist, they have come to be regarded by certain Westerners as deeply spiritual and living in harmony with nature.

Christians who have spent their lives in non-Western cultures—as opposed to those who go on brief visits—have a different perspective on animism. They see it not as harmony with nature but as fear of disaster at the hands of the spirits.

Paul Noren was a missionary kid born in the Belgian Congo. When he was five years old the country won independence and later became Zaire. Paul has lived most of his life there, most recently as a Covenant Church missionary working with the Ngbaka people in agroforestry and fish culture. Paul, Sheryl and their children were spending a year in the United States when Zairian rebels under General Kibula brought down Mobutu Sese Seko's government. When we talked with Paul in April 1997, he did not know when or whether they would be able to return to their beautiful experimental farm. They expected the mission station to be looted by retreating government soldiers. The African head of the Covenant Church was in fact kidnapped by soldiers but released unharmed.

Paul told us of the complications that came up when mission workers wanted to dam a stream and put in a water wheel for a mill:

They believe that if you alter the course of a stream, if you change it and make it work for you, it's going to cost a human life. The water spirits take the life, but the person who does the project somehow "chooses" who will be taken. So when a relative of the mill owner got sick, people accused the owner of sacrificing his relative for the site.

Another time I had trouble getting a certain mason to work on a project. He said he would come to work there after he was convinced that someone had been taken for the project—in other words, someone had died.

Once we diverted water into a grassland for a fish pond. Several people ran off as soon as the water started to flow. They were afraid that something had was going to happen immediately.

Because the people were so afraid of retribution by spirits, an American missionary wondered aloud whether they should be doing these projects at all, or if they were seeming to condone murder. An African Christian responded, "You know we're not killing anybody. The devil wants everyone to be under his power and not go forward."

God Pops Up Everywhere

Other religions and cultures must share the blame for ecological destruction. Still, Christians have to deal with the accusations against our faith. What about the charge that the Bible separates both God and humanity from nature?

Certainly in the Bible God is presented as independent of and other than his creation. He is not part of earth, and earth is not part of him. But he is always here—*separate from* but not *separated from* this world.

In fact people in the Bible spend far more time running from God than they spend searching for him "up there." All through the Bible, God keeps turning up everywhere, especially in places and at times least expected.

Fleeing from his brother Esau and from responsibility in general, Jacob fell into exhausted sleep with a rock for a pillow—hardly a man on a vision quest. In a dream he saw angels going up and down a ladder. But that wasn't all—Jacob saw the Lord. When he woke up he was awestruck, even frightened. "Surely the LORD is in this place, and I was not aware of it," he said to the desert silence. "How awesome is this place! This is none other than the house of God; this is the gate of heaven" (Gen 28:16-17).

Even when people in the Bible try to get away from God, it's a lost cause. One psalmist wrote:

Where can I go from your Spirit?
Where can I flee from your presence?
If I go up to the heavens, you are there;
    if I make my bed in the depths, you are there.
If I rise on the wings of the dawn,
    if I settle on the far side of the sea,
even there your hand will guide me,
    your right hand will hold me fast.
(Ps 139:7-10)

Were the Hebrews High-Tech?

If "dominion" gives free license for the manipulation of nature, history should show us an ancient Hebrew society bustling with industry, busy getting the most out of this creation over which God gave them dominion. After all, the mandate to have dominion over the earth was Hebrew for thousands of years before it was Christian. Bustling industry, however, is exactly what we do not find either in the Bible or in Palestinian archaeology. History looks back to the Romans for their public works projects and to the Greeks for their scientific advances, but it does not look back to the Hebrews for their technological wizardry.

After the Exodus from Egypt, when the Israelites were trekking through the wilderness, their food and drink were credited to the gifts of miraculous manna and water from the rock, not to their cleverness at exploiting the desert. Aaron did have the technical skill to fashion a golden calf-god, but his work is not a bright spot in Jewish history (Ex 32:2-4).

When the Israelites first entered the Promised Land, they were stymied by the people of the plains who had chariots of iron (Judg 1:19). Israel's eventual conquest of Canaan was attributed to God's intervention rather than to superior weaponry. The construction of Moses' tabernacle and Solomon's temple are credited to plans dictated by God rather than to architectural ingenuity. Hiram the metal-working expert, half-Jew and half-Gentile, had to be imported to Jerusalem from Tyre to make the utensils for the temple (1 Kings 7:13-14). In health matters the Hebrews were ahead of their time in diet and cleanliness, but their habits were based on revealed laws of conduct rather than medical research. Hezekiah's water tunnel at Jerusalem (2 Kings 20:20) stands out because it is such an unusual technical accomplishment in Jewish history.

From Old to New
Then is the fault with the reinterpretation of the Old Testament by the New? Is Christian doctrine to blame for distancing God from nature? The accusation does not fit a faith rooted in Incarnation: God in the flesh, God walking in a physical body on this material earth.

According to the Nicene Creed, Jesus is the Savior "by whom all things were made; who for us men, and for our salvation, came down from heaven; and was incarnate by the Holy Ghost of the Virgin Mary, and was made man; and was crucified also for us under Pontius Pilate. He suffered and was buried; and the third day he rose again according to the Scriptures."

God in the New Testament is the opposite of a distant figure uninvolved with the planet. He gets intimately involved with this earth to the ultimate extent. In Jesus, God becomes one of us, the Creator who by choice "became flesh and made his dwelling among us" (John 1:14).

God in the flesh walks the dusty roads, gets tired, gets thirsty, gets irritated, weeps at a graveside, grieves over the self-righteousness of his enemies and the squabbling of his friends. He observes nature closely and uses it in his teaching: soil, seeds, fish, sheep, goats, birds, flowers, trees, the sky, light, water. "The parables of Jesus lifted a veil from the face of Nature; they connect the things of sense to the things of faith."[6] At the end God even experiences physical nature in extremis—he goes through the last thing God should ever go through, physical death.

The Incarnation is a deeper involvement with the material world, a far more profound commitment to this earth, than any god could make who is already "part of the earth."

Real Christian Practice
The early Christians did not get busy exploiting the earth with their

incarnate Savior's blessing. History points in the opposite direction. They refused to buy into the exploitative power structures of the cultures around them.

In the early 1950s, years before the popular environmental movement pointed the finger of ecological blame at Christianity, French sociologist and Catholic layman Jacques Ellul wrote a remarkable critique of the mechanization of culture, titled *La Technique*. It was translated in the 1960s as *The Technological Society*. Ellul wrote of the Christian-dominated Middle Ages in Europe:

> The society which developed from the tenth to the fourteenth century was vital, coherent, and unanimous; but it was characterized by a total absence of the technological will. It was "a-capitalistic" as well as "a-technical." . . . Only architectural technique developed and asserted itself; but this was prompted not by a technical state of mind but by religious impulse.[7]

Today we see a similar impulse in Christian groups who try to get back to the essence of New Testament faith. Their move is always in the direction of simplicity rather than complexity. They reduce their standard of living by retreating to simplified rural life, or, if they live in the city, they share cars and other resources. They are marked by less drive for material wealth, not more. If there is a drive for dominion inherent in basic Christianity, why do these most basic Christians not display it?

We often see the same phenomenon when a materially successful person becomes a Christian. Gadgets and status symbols suddenly become less important and are often disposed of. The person's urge is to get back to the heart of life, to stop acquiring and start divesting because new spiritual values have replaced the old materialistic drive.

The people most surprised to hear that Christianity separates God from nature are those involved with Christian camping, one of the most popular and successful religious efforts of the past generation. The philosophy behind Christian camping is that the natural world is the ideal place to contemplate and encounter God. As young people and sometimes families retreat for a week or two to a rustic setting by a lake—or at least a pond—to study the Bible and worship God, thousands look back to Christian camp as their doorway to a deeper spiritual life.

Caring for the Earth Because We Worship the Creator

Christians of many different persuasions are becoming more active in environmental efforts, and some have been active all along. Only three years after "The Historical Roots of Our Ecologic Crisis" appeared, the number of publications relating the Judeo-Christian tradition to ecology had quadrupled.[8] Several denominations have published statements on the church's responsibility to take care of the earth, and several grassroots Christian organizations have sprung up for education and support of environmental issues. (See "Further Resources" at the back of this book.)

Christians find that they don't have to abandon the Bible to get involved with ecology. The Bible is their guidebook for understanding their responsibility to take care of God's creation. They realize that "The earth is the LORD's, and everything in it, the world, and all who live in it" (Ps 24:1). The Bible has much to say about taking care of land and how closely land use is tied to faith and justice.

For example, when Israel entered Canaan, the Promised Land, they were instructed to let their land lie fallow every seventh year. As the Law provided for a day of rest every seven days for people and animals, the land was to receive a year of rest every seven years, and the people were to trust God to provide for them (Lev 25:1-5). Later the Hebrew prophets like Isaiah, Hosea and Amos cried out against the greed and injustice which brought desolation on the land as well as the poor.

God's Representatives on Earth

What about that bothersome command in Genesis for humanity to have dominion over the earth? It continues to get a lot of bad press. Dominion deserves to be looked at more closely and in its full context in Genesis.

The Hebrew words of Genesis 1:28 are muscular words. "Subdue" is the Hebrew *kabash,* as in our phrase "they really put the kibosh on my idea." To "rule" or "have dominion" is *radah,* meaning to "tread down" or "trample," also to "govern" or "rule."

Nothing wishy-washy about those commands of God to the first humans! But dominion is neither the first nor the last word God spoke about our relationship with the earth. God first said he would make human beings, male and female, in his own image (Gen 1:26).

In ancient times a king would assert his new authority in a conquered country by setting up an image of himself. His image made his presence felt even when he could not be seen in the flesh. Made in God's image, people are meant to be the representatives of God on earth, announcing his lordship and carrying out his will.

After the creation, Genesis goes on to say, "the LORD God took the man and put him in the Garden of Eden to work it and take care of it" (Gen 2:15). To "work" is in Hebrew *abad,* "to till" or "to serve." God did not mean for humanity to serve the land as in serving an idol, but to tend it with a servant's heart. To "take care of" is *shamar,* meaning "to guard or be vigilant for the sake of another." Humanity was always to remember that the garden belonged to God, not to Eve or Adam.

An Ecological Mission

A great deal of ecological work in former European colonies is being done by Christian missionaries—those people often condemned for importing destructive Western ideas. (More about them in chapter six.) Their work doesn't make headlines, but it is helping to make and keep indigenous societies self-sustaining.

An interesting example is the system of self-sustaining fish ponds pioneered by Evangelical Covenant Church missionaries in Thailand. Over 90 percent of the people of northeast Thailand are poor rice farmers. In the fall, after rice harvest, 60 percent must leave to go find work in the city. The yearly exodus disrupts both family life and the hope of building a strong Thai church in the rural areas.

Thai Christians are finding a solution by using their available resources (pigs, ducks, small ponds, grass and fish) in "integrated ecosystem cooperatives." There is a fish pond next to a pig pen. A rice mill provides cracked rice and bran for feed for the pigs and for ducks that swim in the pond. Waste from the pigs and ducks, along with grass, is put into the pond in compost mounds—excellent fertilizer for plankton and other plants that thrive in the sunny pond. Five kinds of fish eat at different levels in the pond, not competing with each other for food. Grass growing at the pond's edge controls erosion and provides food for carp. Dead fish are put into another pond for catfish. The fish thrive and grow large, then are harvested and sold. The aim is to use everything on the cooperative farms and waste as little as possible.

The Covenant Church mission does not own the farmland; the land is owned by a Thai foundation. The farms produce a stable income so farmers don't have to leave their villages each year to work in the city. They encourage spiritual growth through responsibility, service and cooperation. They provide food to keep the people healthy; a church burdened by malnourishment has little energy for ministry. The sustainable fish-pond system is being reproduced in varying forms in other places, such as the Norens' mission station in the former Zaire.

Exploitation Requires Separation

Earlier we saw how anytime God is excluded from any part of life, that area becomes wide open for selfish exploitation—whether in Christian leaders' sexual or financial lives or in how we treat the natural world. In order to exploit anything or anybody with a clear conscience, we must see ourselves living in a universe without a holy God who made us and who has ultimate say in how we live. Then the question becomes, When and where in the history of Western culture did such a split between God and the world come about, so that people began to imagine a universe where the Creator is not actively involved?

In his classic article denouncing European Christianity's "faith in perpetual progress," Lynn White faltered at a vital point. He could not explain why no such "faith in perpetual progress" shows up in the Eastern branch of Christianity, the Orthodox Church, which split off from the Roman Catholic church in the eleventh century:

> What I have said may well apply to the medieval West, where in fact technology made spectacular advances. But the Greek East, a highly civilized realm of equal Christian devotion, seems to have produced no marked technological innovation after the late 7th Century.

During our year living in Ukraine, we occasionally attended services of the Russian Orthodox church. We sometimes asked our university students who were Christians to go with us, hoping they could explain what was going on in the services—but they were almost as mystified as we were. The meanings of the ancient rituals were too obscure for them.

Orthodoxy claims to be true precisely because it has remained fixed and unchanging. To the Orthodox church, progress is not a divine mandate but a threat. The liturgy of worship, the robes of the priests, the chants, the style of art, the rules governing the painting of icons—all continue as they have for centuries. If Christian belief spurs progress and innovation, its effects should show up there too. What accounts for the difference?

In medieval European Christianity, nature provided unquestioned evidence of God's existence, care, love and righteous judgment. The world's grand design and hierarchy spoke of One who made and ruled all creation. All things, from worm to rock to human being to star, were engaged in a celestial dance glorifying their Creator. In the cycle of seasons and the threat of plague and death, people could not escape their daily dependence on their Maker.

In the Renaissance, people looked beyond the church and asked about the world and their place in it. Invention and exploration expanded the perceived limits of human activity. Human will and passion showed in a new artistic naturalism, though its expression was often turned to the service of the church.

The new emphasis on individuality and freedom prepared Europe for the Reformation. Every person was responsible before God, every believer a priest, the way to God open to everyone by faith, the Bible an open book to anyone who could read it. This world was the arena of God's redeeming activity, a place to be brought increasingly under the lordship of Christ.

But soon the doors of the Western mind were closing, swinging shut on the well-oiled hinges of the great universal Machine. A new world view, human-centered and based on natural reason, was spreading across Europe. It put full faith in empirical observations and conclusions drawn by rational and perfectible humans.

Slamming the Doors of the Universe
Pioneering scientist Francis Bacon wrote hopefully in *Novum Organum*

(1620), "Only let the human race recover the right over nature which belongs to it by divine bequest, and let power be given it; the exercise thereof will be governed by sound reason and true religion." As Enlightenment thinking spread across Europe, human power and right over nature were divorced from the Creator and were interpreted as the right to exploit nature for all that could be gotten out of it.

A fraternity of *philosophes*—radical scholars and intellectuals—set out to secularize life and close tight the doors of the universe against divine interference. Gifted writers such as Voltaire mocked Christian faith with cynicism and wit. If all things can be understood through human reason, if there is no such thing as the miraculous, if there is no living God active in human affairs, then Christian faith is a laughable superstition.

Francis Schaeffer summarized the thinking of the times this way:

The utopian dream of the Enlightenment can be summed up by five words: reason, nature, happiness, progress, and liberty. It was thoroughly secular in its thinking. The humanistic elements which had risen during the Renaissance came to flood tide in the Enlightenment. Here was man starting from himself absolutely.[9]

If humanity is the measure of everything, then a personal God who might interfere with human progress—and who might demand accountability for it—is not only a philosophical problem but a pesky nuisance.

The Divine Watchmaker

Of course God can be denied as nonexistent, but nonexistence cannot be proved scientifically. So the Age of Reason ingeniously disposed of God as many people have disposed of God—through religion.

Deism was the religion which got God out of the way. Deism recognizes a Creator God, but this God is a master mechanic who long ago wound up the universe, then left it to run in its self-contained system while he took an extended vacation. The concept of nature as machine and the "freeing" of nature from God led logically to the loosing of all controls over how humans made use of the machine. A moral God demanding justice was replaced by an invisible hand guaranteeing progress.

Though Christians have individual failings in the area of ecological responsibility, it was not Bible-believing Christians who provided the greatest philosophical threat to the sacredness of the earth. It was the leaders of the Enlightenment who pushed God off the world stage, leaving nature unprotected in a world gone secular. God was deported from the universe and installed as a benevolent creator, necessary to get the world going, but with no further business intervening in things.

In the following chapter concerning science we will look more deeply at the effects of the Enlightenment. Meanwhile we can all be honest enough with ourselves to ask whether the Enlightenment view is so different from how we usually think of God, whether we profess Christianity or not.

4/ "Christians Are Antiscientific"

MYTH #4: "Christianity is antiscientific. The church has historically suppressed learning in general and scientific inquiry in particular. Christians even promote pseudoscience by trying to force science to fit a literal interpretation of the Bible."

You don't think much of scientists, do you?
—*Clarence Darrow to William Jennings Bryan at the Scopes "monkey" trial, July 20, 1925*

The phone call was from a stranger inviting us to work with him on a new book project. This book, he assured us, would blow the theory of evolution out of the water. Our caller had learned that Charles Darwin, on his deathbed, recanted his evolutionary doctrines and died a professing Christian.

This was interesting news. We asked the caller for the source of his information. Well, he said, he had heard it from somebody reliable. Did he have documented evidence to back up the story? Maybe a quote from a witness who was with Darwin when he died? Or someone who had talked to a witness? No, he admitted, but he hoped to have something soon.

Our caller's bombshell sounded likely to go *fzzzt*. Still we invited him to contact us again when he got some hard and fast historical evidence.

A few months later he called us back. The Darwin story had turned out to be phony, he said, but would we be interested in working on another project? We passed.

To Think or to Believe?

No wonder evangelical Christians have a reputation for mistrusting, misusing and even disparaging science. Our talks with the anti-Darwin author confirm all the usual negatives:

☐ Christians feel threatened by science's power to erode traditional interpretations of the Bible.

☐ In their zeal to discredit "atheistic" scientists, Christians pounce on any scrap of evidence without caring how reliable it is.

☐ Scientific inquiry demands that people think, but Christians don't want to think; they only want to believe their own preconceived ideas.

Life on Mars—Hell on Earth?

Of course certain Christians take certain scientific developments in stride. They welcome breakthroughs in cancer research and energy efficiency, and they've embraced the Internet with passionate ardor. But it seems religious people circle the wagons every time there's some whopping new revelation about the origin of life or the size of the universe. Take, for example, the possibility of life on other planets.

In the summer of 1996 NASA announced that a meteorite from Mars contained evidence of living organisms. (At least they had been alive several million years ago.) One newspaper columnist enjoyed the thought of how the news must be churning the stomachs of conservative Christians.

Life on Mars will be hell on Earth for Creationists, who already have their hands full trying to turn back the march of science on this planet.

Inerrantists, who believe the Bible is the literal word of God, could be hard-pressed to explain life on Mars. Did the Bible overlook life on Mars, or is the Red Planet part of the firmament?

People who believe the Bible is allegorical have more room to accommodate life on Mars. But everyone whose religion places mankind and Earth at the center of their faith will have to make some accommodation if the discovery proves true.[1]

By that columnist's picture, Christians go through life scared to death that science will disprove the Bible. In the face of every mind-expanding scientific revelation, churchgoers have to either shut their eyes or abandon their beliefs. Usually they wind up clutching their beliefs and denying the discoveries of science.

Separate Realms, Separate Rules?

Critics wish that Christians would relax about science—and they could if they would stop confusing science and religion. Religion is a private zone where a person finds comfort, hope, strength and meaning for life. It deals with matters of belief and faith; it does not provide data for the science lab. Religion is "real" only in the sense that it is real to the believer. Whether it is real in any other sense is (literally) immaterial. By contrast, science deals with fact, not feeling. Science lives in the material world, which we can observe and measure.

Certain Christians, however, don't get this difference. They claim their religion is not only testable in the lab but is rigorously scientific. "Creation scientists," say their opponents, have concocted an odd mix of pseudo-science and Biblical literalism—and the resulting hybrid would be laughable if it didn't threaten to nose its way into state legislatures and school curriculum.

In the professional journal of the National Association of Biology Teachers, Wayne W. Carley did a fresh twist on the dangers of bringing religion into the science classroom. Not only is religion inherently untestable by scientific means, he said, but to test it would be to destroy it:

The real threat to having religion in the science classroom is to the religion, not the science. Evolution can and will stand up to scientific scrutiny over time. But the very testing of religious beliefs such as creationism in a scientific setting destroys the basis of religion: faith. Just as evolution is fundamental to biology, faith is the very foundation of religion. Placing a religious belief under scientific analysis, which demands physical evidence, erodes the faith that is fundamental to that belief.[2]

Beyond Creation Versus Evolution

While in his guest editorial Carley used the word "science" broadly, he used the word "religion" to specifically mean "the current creation-evolution debate." In the popular secular mind, that debate defines the entire battle between Christianity and science.

The creation-evolution debate has high visibility, inspires loud vocal combat and seems custom-made for satire on both sides. As a result, critics of "creation science" often make the mistake of equating one particular interpretation of Genesis with the whole of Christian thought about science. But it isn't fair to either science or Christian faith to substitute one narrow controversy for the larger historic question of what science and faith have to do with one another.

Science encompasses far more than biology or geology or cosmology; today a working scientist might be engaged in meteorology, neonatal medicine, computer technology, genetics or any of hundreds of other fields. And while all Christians believe God is Creator, they are doing serious work in medical ethics, Bible translation, children's moral development, reform of the justice system and hundreds of other areas beyond how and when God created the world.

Some critics of "creation science" leap the gap from condemning Biblical literalism to debunking Christian belief in general. In an article titled "Dumping on Darwin," Michael D. Lemonick critiques that "small, vociferous band of religiously motivated scholars" who "try to discredit evolution by teaching seemingly scientific but subtly Bible-based alternatives." Then—so effortlessly as to require no thought at all—Lemonick makes the macro-leap from questioning a literal reading of Genesis to doubting that the universe shows any hard evidence of intelligent design: "The notion that the world's complexity bespeaks deliberate design is intuitively appealing. But while it's a legitimate religious belief or philosophical speculation, scientists insist it isn't science and shouldn't be taught as such."[3]

An Orderly Universe

Lemonick tells us "scientists insist" that seeing intelligent design in the universe "isn't science." Which scientists is he talking about? Certainly not theistic scientists, a species whom Lemonick has apparently never met. Nor the many scientists before Darwin who saw no conflict between their scientific explorations and the authority of God's Word.

The idea that scientists do not, should not and cannot deal with the possibility of God reflects a comparatively recent turn of scientific dogma. It is not true to the history of science. In fact it was the Christian worldview of an orderly universe, created by an intelligent being, that made modern science possible.

All cultures have explanations of how the world began and what keeps it going. People everywhere have observed the earth and sky and tried to figure out reasons for what they see. But it makes all the difference whether the observer sees nature as predictable and orderly or unstable and erratic.

If the world is controlled by unpredictable spirits, there can be no natural laws because there is no way to tell what is going to happen next. Humans can try to gain the spirits' favor through ritual, but they never know what tricks the gods will play. Even in the sophisticated Greek pantheon, the gods and goddesses were capricious tricksters who played with earthly forces to manipulate human beings.

Scientific curiosity and discovery were part of the historic Greek, Chinese and Islamic cultures, but those cultures did not develop the methods of experimentation and verification which are the basis of the modern scientific method. For example, Greek astronomers by the fourth century B.C. had made important and accurate observations of the stars. Then idealism took the place of empiricism.

The philosophy of Plato (4th century B.C.) and others disdained the visible world and exalted the "real" world of ideas and abstractions. Experimental science was considered by Plato and his disciples to be "mere engineering"—not worth the attention of great intellects.[4]

By contrast, early European scientists such as Copernicus, Kepler and Galileo were committed Christians who saw science as a way to know and glorify God. They believed nature and Scripture were equally God's revelation; both were needed to better understand the Creator.

The Galileo Story

How can Galileo and God be mentioned in the same paragraph? Wasn't Galileo hounded by the church until he was forced to recant his heretical view that the earth revolved around the sun? Doesn't he symbolize the martyrdom of free scientific inquiry at the hands of oppressive religion?

Galileo Galilei—astronomer, mathematician, inventor, debater—was an outspoken critic of the Italian academic establishment of his day, especially of their Aristotelian views. In the late sixteenth and early seventeenth centuries, the Aristotelian model of the universe ruled university thinking. The universe is finite; it is spherical; the earth is at the center; the physics of heavenly bodies is different from the physics of earth.

When Galileo used his telescopic observations to disprove Aristotle's model of the universe, his enemies turned to theology and the church to defeat him. Charles E. Hummel's study of the church and science gives a constellation of details of the thirty-year controversy that culminated in 1633. He concludes that Galileo "saw no need for a breach between science and theology since God is the Author of both books—of nature and of Scripture. If the church were to forbid anything, it should be the imposition of scriptural authority in scientific debates, which should be settled by experience and reason."[5]

The split between science and Christian faith began not with Galileo but a century later, with the philosophers of the Enlightenment who endeavored to push God out of the universe.

The Absent Watchmaker

The emerging conflict in the eighteenth century was not between Christianity and science but between Christianity and *naturalistic* science, which writes God out of the picture before the discussion begins. To the leaders of the Enlightenment, God was a divine watchmaker who had constructed the cosmos according to certain laws and then left it to run on its own.

An absent God is an open invitation for science to explore the empty cosmic machination with no regard for right and wrong. As we saw in the preceding chapter, it is license to *exploit* the great machine as well. Morality and other theological questions become irrelevant. The cosmic machine becomes the only proper field of human inquiry, because beyond the machine we can know nothing.

In *Critique of Pure Reason,* Immanuel Kant (1724-1804) held that the only knowledge available to humanity is that which can be gotten through the senses. He left no room for the possibility of revealed or supernatural knowledge.

> Buoyed by favorable response to his supposed achievement, [Kant] proceeded to knock down, through circular reasoning, Augustine's and Aquinas's "irrefutable" arguments for God's existence. . . . Kant's ideas not only began to dominate cosmology and impact theology, but they shaped the thinking that spawned many of the "isms" of the nineteenth and twentieth centuries.[6]

A few centuries after Kant, J. P. Moreland, professor of philosophy at Talbot School of Theology, was rebuffed by a physics professor at a dinner party. "On learning that I was a philosopher and theologian," Moreland says, "he informed me of the irrational nature of my fields, contending that science had removed the need to believe in God."[7]

Wading In Recklessly

Moreland's accuser was speaking as a true scientific naturalist. But what's wrong with that? Shouldn't a true scientist be a naturalist as far as his or her work is concerned? Isn't the possibility of the existence of God—in fact, of anything having to do with the supernatural—totally outside the realm of science? Doesn't science properly deal with the material world only and have nothing to do with theological questions?

Technically, yes. That's why "creation scientists" get accused of intellectual dishonesty. They are seen as theologians in disguise who wade recklessly into science with their supernatural agenda. At the same time, some supposedly materialistic scientists wade just as recklessly into theology by making daring statements—absolute statements—about the nonmaterial world.

When the late Carl Sagan intoned "The cosmos is all that is or ever was or ever will be," he stepped outside the bounds of material science to make a brazenly theistic—or rather antitheistic—pronouncement. He was declaring not only that the cosmos exists (there is a natural reality) but that nothing exists *outside* the cosmos (there is no supernatural reality). Sagan reminds us that not all statements made by scientists are scientific statements. His proclamation that only the cosmos exists may have been his personal conviction or his intuitive feeling; it could not be called a statement of scientific fact.

If science deals only with the material world, it's not fair for science to make statements about the nonmaterial world. When they do, they're playing on both teams at once while claiming that one team has to forfeit because it didn't show up.

The Board of Directors of the National Association of Biology Teachers did just that in 1995 when they adopted a set of twenty "tenets of science, evolution and biology education." The twentieth tenet is this:

Science and religion differ in significant ways that make it inappropriate to teach any of the different religious beliefs in the science classroom.[8]

The NABT declares that science teachers can't deal with "God" issues in the classroom; they can't mix science and religion, and if they try, it's bad science. But if we go back to the head of the list, we find something fascinating. Here's the first of their twenty tenets:

The diversity of life on earth is the outcome of evolution: an unsupervised, impersonal, unpredictable and natural process of temporal descent with genetic modification that is affected by natural selection, chance, historical contingencies and changing environments.[9]

In other words, there has been absolutely nothing and nobody on the outside of the system making evolution happen. Like Sagan, the NABT makes an audacious theistic—actually, antitheistic—statement. It's radically different from saying "We don't know if anybody caused this." It says "We do know, and nobody did."

In recent years Berkeley law professor Phillip Johnson has been engaged in lively, good-natured questioning of naturalistic science and its right to dominate education. He explains how nontheistic scientists make religion irrelevant by putting religion in the category of the irrational: "It is said that naturalism is science, whereas theism belongs to religion; naturalism is based on reason, whereas theism is based on faith; and naturalism provides knowledge, whereas theism provides only belief. Science, reason and knowledge easily trump religion, faith and belief."[10]

Two Kinds of Science

So are Christianity and science in conflict with each other? Yes and no. Are they compatible? Yes and no.

True biblical Christianity is fully compatible with intellectually honest, open-minded science which takes into account the possibility that there is Something or Someone besides this physical universe, a reality independent from the universe yet intimately involved with it.

Christianity and naturalistic science, however, are always going to lock horns. Christianity and naturalism are based on two different concepts of reality. When the issue gets down to what's rational and what's irrational, what's real and what's unreal, the conflict can reach gut level.

The editor of the professional journal *The American Biology Teacher,* Randy Moore, feels slapped in the face by certain students in his introductory biology class. No wonder. Not only do they insist on believing in a Creator, they also tell him the earth is only 6,000 years old and he is "a pagan who will burn in hell" if he doesn't repent of teaching evolution.

Well, the best of us would bristle if we were called pagans who will burn in hell. Moore shoots back that creationism "represents arbitrary faith and is an outward sign of ignorance and anti-intellectualism." His sarcastic editorial goes on to link creationists in an imaginary future alliance with "psychics, astrologers, UFO chasers, spell casters, tarot card readers, Bigfoot believers, numerologists, faith healers, channelers, spoon benders, crystal feelers, Elvis spotters and Ouija board readers."[11]

Ouch. Unless this teacher is exaggerating, there are some Christian biology students out there who need to learn some tact. At the same time, mockery and name-calling of creationists isn't scientifically objective either. Whatever is going on here, it's as far from real science as our caller was when he got the unsubstantiated goods on Darwin.

Bunk on Both Sides

Even superstar paleontologist Stephen J. Gould recognized that scientists can be biased and that their theories tend to validate prevailing worldviews: "Scientists, as ordinary human beings, unconsciously reflect in their theories the social and political constraints of their times. As privileged members of society, more often than not they end up defending existing social arrangements as biologically foreordained."[12]

Example: A daring new mass-extinction hypothesis was published in 1984 by University of Chicago paleontologists David Raup and Jack Sepkoski Jr. They proposed that chunks of comets periodically smash into earth, causing devastating environmental shocks. The dinosaurs were victims of a massive comet crack-up. There were others in the more distant past and we can expect more to come—about one every twenty-six million years.

In the midst of the riot of debate over the theory, which was outlandish by conventional scientific wisdom, Dr. Raup wrote his brief book *The Nemesis Affair*. He called the book "a fail-safe strategy. If the whole research program came tumbling down, I could describe its history as scientific discovery gone wrong."[13] While cheerfully admitting that his theory could be mistaken, Raup demonstrated how the scientific community resists "maverick ideas."[14]

[W]orking scientists are subject to many more prejudices and preconceptions than is generally thought. . . . Most scientists argue that religion is not science because religion involves no experiments, tests no hypotheses, and is committed beforehand to a set of beliefs. Science and faith are antithetical. It follows that scientific research is objective because the scientist is not influenced by prior expectations and is willing to let the chips fall where they may. I think these statements contain a fair amount of bunk.[15]

Raup said there is bunk in the idea that science is always objective. As a scientist dealing with scientists, he was in a position to know. And Christians are in a position to know that there is bunk on both sides of the conflict.

Another example: An electrifying story made the rounds in international Christian circles that an oil-well-drilling crew had broken through a massive hole in the earth from which terrific heat boiled out. The crew lowered a microphone into the hole and heard the screams of lost souls. They had broken through into hell!

The story was a stunner because it appeared to prove that hell exists deep inside the earth and that people are actually confined there. It was told and retold and accepted by many Christians who read it. The problem was: no one could ever trace the story to a definite factual source. Where was this oil drilling site? What were the names of the crew? Where are their firsthand statements recorded? Why didn't the microphone melt? Those who took the tale at face value were uninterested in checking out hard facts. It was enough that the story validated what they wanted to be true.

Who's Right? or What's True?

Both Christians and nonbelievers get caught up in the lust to vindicate ourselves and humiliate the enemy. While we all claim we're engaged in the pursuit of truth, the pursuit of truth often gets lost in the drive to prove that we're right and the other side is wrong. The drive unites the most atheistic scientist and the most fundamentalist Christian. We are both too busy asking "Who's right?" when we ought to be asking "What's true?"

"What's true?" is a valid scientific and theological query. "Who's right?" is a debate over human power.

If we look under the surface of science-religion conflicts, from the seventeenth-century trial of Galileo to the twentieth-century Scopes "monkey" trial, they are primarily about neither science nor faith. They are about control. They are fought over who will decide what is taught in the universities or the school classrooms and who will have the ultimate authority to dictate what people believe.

The Monkey Trial

Evolution versus the old-time religion. Clarence Darrow versus William Jennings Bryan. The stereotypical view of the 1925 Scopes trial is that a progressive science teacher dared to teach evolution and got persecuted by flat-earth fundamentalists. The trial drove a wedge between science and religion in the public mind for decades to come. But did it really prove that science and the Bible are incompatible?

The Tennessee law for which a young high school teacher agreed to be indicted had been on the books only four months. The law itself did not mention evolution by name. It made it "unlawful" for teachers in state-supported schools "to teach the theory that denies the story of the divine creation of man as taught in the Bible, and to teach instead that man has descended from a lower order of animals."[16] Dr. George Rappleyea of Dayton, whose (human) ancestors had suffered religious persecution in France, decided to test the law's constitutionality in court.[17]

A key legal issue was whether the state of Tennessee had interfered with religious freedom by mandating a particular interpretation of the Bible. Several science professors were ready to testify in John Scopes's defense. They were professing Christians, active in their churches, and they planned to appeal to the Bible in their testimony.[18]

Modernist clergymen at the turn of the century actually welcomed Darwin's theory of evolution because it flattered humanity and implied that the human race could only get better. If life evolved from lower forms to higher, then humanity is the peak of the evolutionary process. And if upward progression is written into the very nature of things, then progress is inevitable—a tenet of the industrial age. Embracing Darwinism was a way to keep the church in the cultural mainstream and prevent Christianity from getting left in the dust of folklore. The established church did not want to repeat the Galileo fiasco by standing against science and being proved embarrassingly wrong.

Meanwhile the more conservative churches of the day had withdrawn into the fortress of Biblical literalism. Their standard became "The Bible says it, I believe it, and that settles it"—expressed not as confidence in Scripture but as fear of anything which threatened their interpretations of Scripture.

On the seventh day of the trial, the proceedings were moved outdoors because of the heat and the crowds.[19] On the courthouse lawn, in a dramatic maneuver, the defense team led by attorney Clarence Darrow put prosecutor William Jennings Bryan on the stand as a witness for the defense because Bryan was considered an expert on the Bible. Darrow proceeded to storm Bryan's stronghold of biblical literalism; Bryan held the fort. It was "a heated, two-hour exchange that, in the end, did not affect the case as much as it did the nation."[20] Both men wound up on their feet shouting and shaking their fists at each other while Judge Raulston banged his gavel.[21] It made great outdoor summer theater, but it hardly helped anyone find the truth about either the Bible or science.

In the end "the fundamentalists convinced the jury but not the larger American public. At best, the trial revealed that even among American Christians in the 1920s, there were two competing standards for determining truth, one 'biblical,' the other 'scientific,' and it was difficult to see how they could be reconciled."[22] The Scopes trial did more than polarize evolutionists versus Bible literalists. It also polarized moderate Christians, forcing them toward the extremes of two camps, modernist or fundamentalist.

Two Volumes, One Briefcase

The 1955 stage play *Inherit the Wind,* loosely based on the Scopes trial, ends with a powerful symbolic act. Henry Drummond, the character based on Darrow, has just received word of the death of Matthew Brady, the character based on Bryan. Left alone in the courtroom, Drummond picks up a copy of Darwin's *Origin of Species* in one hand and a Bible in the other hand. He looks from one to the other while the audience wonders which book he will choose. Then he "slaps the two books together and jams them in his brief case, side by side" and makes his exit.[23]

There's no evidence Clarence Darrow ever did or would do such a thing. But could the symbolic act work in reality? Can the Bible and a book of science fit side by side on a shelf or in an inquiring human mind? Or will there always be incompatibility and conflict?

Many Christians in the sciences say their observation of the material world leads them toward faith, not away from it. They embrace science as their life's work while they live their lives by faith—their total lives, not simply one religious compartment. They feel no need to shut their eyes to truth or pretend to live in two worlds with two different sets of rules.

Faith is never an excuse for sloppy science. A scientist who is a Christian has no right to say "It's a miracle!" every time an experiment in the lab fails to yield the expected results. But a scientist who believes in a good and compassionate Creator can't help taking the Creator into account in any observations of the physical world. This is "theistic science":

> rooted in the idea that Christians ought to consult all they know—including theological beliefs—in forming and testing hypotheses, in explaining things in science, and in evaluating the plausibility of scientific theories.
>
> More specifically, theistic science expresses a commitment to the belief that God, conceived of as a personal agent with great power and intelligence, has through direct, primary causation and indirect, secondary causation created and designed the world for a purpose.[24]

Dr. Hugh Siefken, a nuclear physicist who teaches at Greenville College, an evangelical Christian college in Illinois, looks at it this way: "My faith can be summed up in this one paradox: I believe in science, and I believe in God. I plan to continue testifying to both."[25] He goes on to explain something of his spiritual and scientific journey:

> Some of my personal beliefs about God have remained absolutely fixed over the years, and in other ways I've grown to appreciate His work even more. . . . While none of us have it all figured out—not even physicists—I've seen enough to conclude with confidence that the universe was designed by a supreme being.[26]

Design and Beginnings

Contrary to the "creation versus evolution" stereotype, there is no single monolithic Christian opinion about the age of the earth or when life began on earth, the size of the universe, the "big bang," the possibility of change in life forms over time or whether there is life on other planets. If the outsider's view is that Christians hide behind walls, then behind those walls there is a lot of lively scientific debate going on.

Dr. Siefken prefers to direct the focus away from when the world was created to who created it:

> Heaven is not going to be lost or gained by whether one believes in a six-day creation model. Of more importance for me is acknowledging the one who set it all in motion and continues to sustain it.[27]

While the precise age of the earth or time of creation are endlessly and perhaps futilely debated, Christian and non-Christian scientists agree that the basic issues of design and beginnings are the crucial points where science meets the possibility of God. Atheistic scientists betray the importance of the issues of design and beginnings when they get uncomfortable with any evidence of either, and when they make strong pronouncements that these questions have no place in science. Dr. Siefken theorizes about the discomfort:

> Physicists in general are very sure of themselves. It's probably because they understand so much of the physical world. They can explain it and work it out mathematically. For this reason, they often tend to exclude religious notions in their discipline. They think, Why do I need God?
>
> But the one thing they haven't figured out is how it all got started. What was there before the big bang? No physicist can get all the way back to time zero. . . . So we're left with the question of what—or who—caused it to begin.[28]

Beyond Testing

Naturalistic scientists become uneasy at the point of the big bang, because if they cannot say for sure what was there or what happened before the beginning of the universe, that leaves the door wide open for a creator. Some scientists state very explicitly their reluctance—even fear—of leaving that door open. British astronomer Sir Fred Hoyle found it more philosophically appealing to believe in the steady-state theory that the universe had no beginning:

> This possibility [steady state] seemed attractive, especially when taken in conjunction with aesthetic objections to the creation of the universe in the remote past. For it seems against the spirit of scientific enquiry

to regard observable effects as arising from 'causes unknown to science,' and this in principle is what creation-in-the-past implies.[29]

Theoretical physicist Michio Kaku wrote about the hottest new area of physics research, quantum cosmology, which theorizes not one big bang but "a constant genesis, or boiling of universes, in an ocean of cosmic nothing or Nirvana." When Kaku proposed this picture to Nobel laureate Steve Weinberg, Weinberg had this reaction:

> I find this an attractive picture. . . . An important implication is that there wasn't a beginning; that there were increasingly larger big bangs, so that the [multiverse] goes on forever—one doesn't have to grapple with the question of it before the bang. The [multiverse] has just been here all along. I find that a very satisfying picture.[30]

Attractive . . . satisfying . . . but true? Kaku admits that "there is no experimental proof for quantum cosmology," but he adds hopefully that "the theory is so compelling and beautiful that it has become the center of intense research."[31] But what kind of research is this, if it cannot test the data and does not care if the data can be tested?

Communication Would Help

Certainly there are aspects of Christian faith which cannot be put under the microscope. But there are aspects of current science which cannot be put under the microscope either. The Christian who says "the Bible says it; that settles it" places his or her version of reality in a safe, sterile realm beyond questioning or testing. So does the materialistic scientist who declares that the universe had no beginning because that's a beautiful and satisfying idea. Neither one is doing very good science.

It is fascinating how two arch-rivals, two "opposites," can share the same position, stand on the same ground, and not realize it. Like Bryan and Darrow, proponents of naturalistic science and proponents of the Bible are still shouting and shaking their fists at each other, going all out to win the case, neither one listening to the other.

Better communication among Christian and non-Christian scientists would help. Phillip Johnson sets an excellent example as he welcomes challenges to his own challenge of naturalism and openly discusses and debates in secular forums. What better way for Christians to understand how scientists can look at the universe and not see the hand of the Creator than to talk to some of them? And vice versa for nontheistic scientists who can't understand how serious scientists can involve Christianity in their studies.

In the course of working on this chapter we have been privileged to talk with several scientists who are sincere Christians. We have listened to them talk about their work and their faith, sometimes late into the night. They invariably explain how they see evidence of God's design in the material world which they examine every day. But there is always more. The discussion moves from the clinical to the personal. These are people for whom this God, this Creator, has done something astounding which they could never deserve. God is not just the one who put this universe here. He is also with them every day. He has offered them forgiveness and connection with himself. They believe he has done that in the real physical world in real history, becoming a human being in Jesus Christ, and he continues to do it in the here and now. And all their study could never have made it happen. For all these scientists, their intellect is tempered and graced by humility.

An Open Heart

We talked with Andrew Chiu, a practicing cardiologist who was born in the United States to Taiwanese immigrant parents. His grandparents were Buddhists; his parents were converted to Catholicism by Jesuit missionaries in China, but they left the church when they came to the United States, where both were university faculty members. Chiu told us,

For me the last step of faith was very hard. What is absolute proof? I don't think it exists. I came at Christianity from an antagonistic point of view. Yet the more I studied it, the more it sounded plausible. It spoke of truth on a completely different level than science. Jesus' sacrifice was a great act of love, and that spoke of higher truth. When I first heard the gospel and the life of Christ, it struck me as one of the most profound . . .

His voice trailed off before he continued:

The most cherished thing scientists have to give up is a mankind-centered universe. I was always impressed by the power of science and what it could accomplish in a material sense in the world around us. Every time I looked in a microscope it absolutely amazed me. How could this have happened by chance? The more I came into contact with Christians and the more times I heard the gospel, the more attractive it sounded. My heart was open, but faith is given by God.

Chiu sees no conflict between faith and science "so long as you recognize the limitations of science and stay humble about it. Some have made science their God. But do we necessarily inhabit a better world today than that which existed six hundred or seven hundred years ago? The human condition now looks like constant repeats of the same old stuff but on a grander scale. Science is a powerful tool—but it does not provide the whole answer."

Purpose Behind the Design

Dr. Paul Anderson, Professor of Biochemistry and Molecular Biology in the School of Medicine at the University of Minnesota—Duluth, says he was first challenged with the spiritual aspect of life in graduate school by a renowned carbohydrate biochemist. While Anderson's professional and personal life were blossoming, he experienced an emptiness which success could not fill. Yet he never felt a conflict between his scientific interest and his curiosity about God. His scientific interest, far from pushing him away from faith, actually made him more open to seeing evidence for God's existence.

The desire for spiritual understanding was amplified by the beauty, order and design evident in the world I observed as a scientist. It was my view that there was a Creator and meaning and purpose behind the design of the natural world and our very existence.[32]

Later in his Christian experience, Dr. Anderson began to wonder why he didn't jump into the public controversies over supposed conflicts between science and religion. When he and several Christian friends in the academic community talked about it, he realized that "it was science that had propelled me in the direction of faith. Why then should I find the two to be in discord?"

Of course, there are very important and interesting issues to address in the relationship between science and faith. But Christian faith has, for me, provided the foundation for answers to such questions as "What is the meaning of life; why are we here?" and "How is life to be lived?" and "What are the values and morals which guide a peaceful society?"—it is not in the province of science to provide answers for such questions.[33]

The scientists we've quoted and many others testify to how Christianity and their scientific inquiry fit together. Are their words valuable beyond expressions of personal opinion?

Playing Fair with the Evidence

In his editorial quoted previously, Wayne W. Carley makes the case that science can be tested and religion cannot; in fact to test religion would be to destroy it. "Even Jesus recognized this principle," he says, and goes on to explain:

> When the disciple Thomas demanded to place his hands in Jesus' wounds before he would believe Jesus had risen, Jesus did not praise Thomas for his wise use of the scientific method. Rather, Jesus praised those of faith, saying, "Blessed are those who have not seen and yet have come to believe" (Jn 20:29; NRSV).[34]

People familiar with the Gospel of John will realize that Carley is not playing fair with the context of Jesus' encounter with Thomas. Thomas had been absent when the other disciples saw Jesus alive and he "showed them his hands and side" (Jn 20:20). But when Thomas expressed a demand for evidence, Jesus came to them again and said specifically to Thomas, "Put your finger here; see my hands. Reach out your hand and put it into my side. Stop doubting and believe" (Jn 20:27).

If that was not an invitation to examine the physical evidence that Jesus was alive, what was it? Thomas was not invited to contemplate a vision of Jesus suspended in the clouds. Jesus offered him data—the best evidence, his own body—and challenged Thomas to evaluate it firsthand. Thomas the questioner was told to stick his finger right into jagged holes made by spikes hammered into a man's wrists as impassively as you nail a sign to a post. Thomas the doubter was urged to thrust his hand into the gash made by a Roman spear jabbed into Jesus' side to make sure he was really dead.

Jesus did pronounce a blessing on people who have never seen his resurrected body yet believe in him. That describes most of the millions of people who have ever believed in him. But those millions have had other kinds of evidence.

How do we even know that Jesus said what he said to Thomas—or said anything else attributed to him in the four Gospels? The study of textual evidence for the Bible can occupy a scholar for a lifetime. There are over 5,000 pieces of ancient manuscript copies of the New Testament, including a scrap of a copy of the Gospel of John dating to approximately 100 years after Jesus' death.[35] The consistency of the biblical record with other historical records attests to its accuracy. The Gospel writer Luke carefully placed Jesus' birth and baptism in their historical context (Lk 2:1-2; 3:1-2). Ancient historians such as Josephus and Pliny the Younger mention Jesus the Christ, supporting the accuracy of the Gospel accounts.

For years we have enjoyed the magazine *Biblical Archaeology Review.* It comes not from a fundamentalist Christian slant but from a rather secular Jewish viewpoint. When *BAR* publishes news of a seal with the name of the prophet Jeremiah's scribe Baruch,[36] or the family tomb of the high priest Caiaphas who tried Jesus,[37] or an inscription which possibly refers to King David,[38] it is showing us touchable physical evidence of biblical people and events. Those finds are not absolute proof of anything—and the editors of *BAR* enjoy nothing more than a good controversy over what a particular find means—but they are pieces of data which can be examined and studied.

Our Way or Somebody Else's?

Asking "What's true?" instead of "Who's right?" makes possible a candid examination of evidence and discussion of implications. The scientist with an open desire for truth, with no preconceived agenda, and the Christian, in complete confidence that all truth is God's truth, both have complete freedom to pursue truth wherever it leads. The ideal is that the two should be combined in the same person.

Of all people, Christians who know God and believe the Bible should be the freest to pursue truth wherever it leads. They can have complete confidence that all truth is God's truth and that he has expressed that truth in the Bible and all of creation.

But neither Christian nor atheist can ever hope to comprehend the truth about the universe and life until each is willing to accept any part of truth which is held by the other. Both sides agree that the possibility of intelligent design and a beginning to the universe are intriguing issues implying some connection between science and theology. Until we both agree to talk about these things in an open and equitable way, we will never get beyond the fist-shaking and shouting.

Genuine scientific inquiry and honest theology both need to recognize the limitations of human knowledge. As Christian believers and nonbelievers discuss the relationship of science and faith, we should do it in the spirit of something said in that Tennessee courtroom immediately after the conviction of John Thomas Scopes. The words were said not by the agnostic defense counsel, Clarence Darrow, but by the fundamentalist prosecutor, William Jennings Bryan:

> I think, my friends and your Honor, that if we are actuated by the spirit that should actuate every one of us, no matter what our views may be, we ought not only desire but pray that that which is right will prevail, whether it be our way or somebody else's.[39]

5/ "Christians Have Done Terrible Things in the Name of Christ"

MYTH #5: "Look at the wrongs that have been done in the name of Christianity—everything from the Crusades to televangelist scandals."

I have seen too many frightful proofs in court—
the Devil is alive in Salem,
and we dare not quail to follow
where the accusing finger points!
—Rev. John Hale in Arthur Miller's "The Crucible"

The workshop was titled "Spiritual Distress." Our hospital chaplain, a former priest now married, was talking about the power of religion—not only its power to support and heal, but its power to hurt and disappoint.

"If you're going to get any help from religion," he said, "you have to realize that it's one-half people, and that's what screws it up."

He continued:

There's no use for religion except as it nourishes our spiritual life. But so often it becomes manipulation. Religion gives people a chance to get hold of and use other people's vulnerability. Many people stop attending to their spiritual lives because they get hurt by religion.[1]

Our Own Hearts, Our Own Histories

A newspaper columnist, griping about warning labels on music albums, began his argument with the accusation "In the 1800s the Puritans burned witches."[2] Like that columnist, many of Christianity's accusers are fuzzy on the historic details but positive of the facts: Christianity has been involved in some awful stuff.

Most of us don't need to look to the great religious oppressions of the past—the Crusades, the Inquisition, the Salem witch trials—to find evidence of hurtful things done in the name of Christ. We need to look only as far as our own hearts and our own histories.

It happens all the time. We get hurt in church. We see others hurt in church. Our connection with church can be broken forever by lawsuits between Christians, unforgiveness, extramarital affairs by pastors, financial misdealings, gossip, power plays or a mystifying spirit of condemnation for actions we don't think are sins. A lot of people have sworn they'll never go near a church again because of what was done to them by so-and-so, who was such an upstanding church member. And if we're honest, we have to admit we have also dealt others pain in our drive to accomplish things which seemed right and spiritual at the time. Unwittingly or deliberately we have been part of that "one-half" who screw things up.

Tyranny and Bloodshed

Of course there are bigger historic wrongs done in the name of Jesus. "Overt tyranny and bloodshed fill the greatest part of religious history," says an atheist home page, and not to leave us guessing about which religion they mean, they zero in on Christianity:

> [T]he killing of heretics became a basic church doctrine during the rule of the Roman Emperor Constantine in the fourth century. Killing in the name of God was a widespread and common practice within Christianity ever since that time, till the last of the witch hunts in the early 1700s. Bloodshed in the name of the Christian religion included the killing of pagan scholars and the burning of their libraries, the Crusades and other holy wars fought to fulfill biblical prophecies, and the reign of terror known as the Inquisition.[3]

We have lived in Northern Ireland, where Protestants and Catholics clashing over political control plant bombs and shoot from rooftops in the name of religion. We have also lived in the former Soviet Union, where for seventy years terrible things were done in the name of freedom from religion. It's only fair to explore both phenomena and see where they lead.

The Crusades

Beginning in the seventh century, fired by a militaristic spirit, Islam took with the sword virtually every place on earth except Europe where Christianity had ruled. Particularly offensive to the church was the fact that all the sacred Holy Land sites of Christian pilgrimages came under Muslim control. At the same time there was a widening split between the two branches of the Christian church—the Western (Roman Catholic, centered in Rome) and Eastern (Orthodox, centered in Constantinople or Byzantium). The formal break came in 1054 when the Patriarch of Constantinople was excommunicated.

When the Seljuk Turks threatened the Byzantine Empire, the Eastern church appealed to the West for help. In 1095, speaking at the Council of Clermont in southern France, Pope Urban II called on Christians to unite and free the Holy Land from the Turks, "an accursed race, a race utterly alienated from God."

> O most valiant soldiers, descendants of invincible ancestors, be not degenerate. Let all hatred between you depart, all quarrels end, all wars cease. Start upon the road to the Holy Sepulchre, to tear that land from the wicked race and subject it to yourselves.[4]

The shouted answer of the crowd, "Deus vult!"—"God wills it!"—became the battle cry of the Crusaders. The time was right for recruiting an army of religious adventurers. The beginning of the second millennium after Christ was "a difficult time in many parts of Europe, where crops had failed and disease ran rampant. Therefore, the call to go to a foreign land as soldiers of Christ was received with enthusiasm by many, both of the lower classes and of the nobility."[5]

The Crusades joined together two themes which were developing strongly in eleventh-century Europe; the holy war, or military expedition blessed by the church, and the pilgrimage to a holy place. The journey of a Christian army to recover the Holy Land from the Muslims fulfilled both of these.[6]

If high adventure, escape from difficult conditions and a holy calling weren't enough incentive to go fight the infidels in Jerusalem, Pope Urban II promised salvation for any who died in the enterprise:

All who go thither and lose their lives, be it on the road or on the sea, or in the fight against the pagans, will be granted immediate forgiveness for their sins. This I grant to all who will march, by virtue of the great gift which God has given me.[7]

The first wave of Crusaders which set out for Jerusalem was a "disorganized mob" and came to disaster.

Along the way, they fed on the land, on which they fell like locusts, and had to fight other Christians who defended their goods and crops. They also practiced their war against the infidel by killing thousands of Jews.[8]

The first formal Crusade battled its way across Asia Minor and eventually took Jerusalem from the Muslims in July 1099. What followed was "a horrible bloodbath."

All the defenders were killed, as well as many civilians. Women were raped and infants thrown against walls. Many of the city's Jews had taken refuge in the synagogue, and the crusaders set fire to the building with them inside. According to an eyewitness, at the Porch of Solomon horses waded in blood.[9]

Jerusalem changed hands several times over the next century, while the Crusades continued in the form of "a regular stream of soldiers, pilgrims and merchants"[10] until about the year 1270. The tragic Children's Crusades, initiated in the belief that God would honor innocence, ended in death or slavery for masses of children.

If the Crusades failed to permanently liberate the Holy Land from the Muslims, they did finalize the split between the Roman Catholic and Orthodox Churches and bring about renewed interest in the person of Jesus and the Bible. Dissension rose against the established church, and leaders of the threatened church responded very humanly by asserting their ecclesiastical power and beginning to actively seek out and punish heresy.

The Beginnings of Inquisition

In the middle of the twelfth century Pope Alexander III "suggested that lay and clerical informers who brought reports of heretics should be supplemented by officials who went out to discover evidence of heresy." Alexander III's successor, Lucius III, decreed that "bishops should take action against heretics."

A special characteristic of this decree, establishing the bishops' inquisition, which was echoed in a contemporary imperial edict, was that a suspect, once convicted of being a heretic, was to be handed over to the secular arm for punishment. The death penalty was not yet official, although medieval heretics had been burned at the stake—often by mobs of lay people—at least from the early eleventh century.[11]

Inquisition proceedings were secret, with the inquisitor in complete authority. The suspect did not know the names of the accusers and was allowed no defense attorney. Torture was used to obtain confessions. The method of attack was swift and merciless:

The inquisitor or his vicar would arrive suddenly, deliver a sermon to the townspeople calling for reports of anyone suspected of heresy, and for all who felt heresy within themselves to come forth and confess, within a period of grace. This was the "general inquisition." When the period of grace expired, the "special inquisition" began, with a summons to suspected heretics who were detained until trial.[12]

Those who did not repent faced death at the stake. "This the Inquisition entrusted to the secular authorities, which pronounced and carried out the sentence, since the church could not shed blood."[13]

Don't Judge by a Masquerade

In the twelfth century St. Bernard described the miserable state of what passed for the body of Christ on earth:

The Church is left poor and bare and miserable, neglected and bloodless. Her children seek not to bedeck, but to spoil her; not to guard her, but to destroy her; not to defend, but to expose; not to institute, but to prostitute; not to feed the flock, but to slay and devour it. They exact the price of sins and give no thought to sinners.[14]

Who would want to identify with a religion like that? The question is whether that religion is true Christianity or some pitiful corrupted imitation of the real thing.

None of us would want our character judged on the basis of an impersonator doing a bad masquerade. For that matter we wouldn't even want ourselves judged by the work of a master impostor. We would want the chance to appear in person, present our authentic selves and be judged on the basis of who we really are.

In the same way it is not fair to judge a religion by a pretense or counterfeit of that religion. Modern Catholics admit that by the time of the Inquisition the church had drifted far from the teachings and practices of Christ and the apostles. And if Catholics are still haunted by the corruption of the medieval church, Protestants in North America are still haunted by their own peculiar ghost in Puritan garb: the Salem witchcraft trials.

Were There Really Witches?

Long before Puritanism, in the shadow of the power of the medieval church in Europe, there were people who practiced the rituals of pre-Christian religions, trafficking with spirits and making use of magic spells. German scholar Jacob Grimm describes how in the thirteenth century the church bore down on the heresy of the old religions:

> Even in the less offensive teaching and practice of some heretics there could not fail to be a mixture of heathen things with christian; the church's zeal had to bestir itself at once against new errors of doctrine and against remnants of heathenism that were combined with them.[15]

These days there are two popular lines of defense for the witches who were condemned by the church. Either they were keepers of the ancient earth religions which the church was compelled to suppress to retain its power, or they were herbalists whose only crime was practicing alternative medicine.

In the anticommunist fervor of the years following World War II, the term "witch hunt" took on a new meaning for Americans. Playwright Arthur Miller watched his fellow artists being called before the House Un-American Activities Committee to answer for their communist leanings of twenty years earlier. In time Miller would be summoned himself.

As a metaphor of the HUAC activities and for his own emotional working out of the conflict, he conceived the idea of writing a play on the Salem witchcraft trials. He went to the source, spending day after cold rainy day in the Salem, Massachusetts, courthouse reading the original records of the 1692 trials. The result was his play "The Crucible."

Miller's associates repeatedly told him that his HUAC/Salem metaphor didn't hold up. After all, real Communists existed; real witches didn't. Through his research, however, Miller (a nonreligious Jew) became convinced of two factors at the root of the Salem trials. First, something more than hysterical imagination lay behind the accusations of sorcery. In his autobiography he wrote:

> I had no doubt that Tituba, Reverend Parris's black Barbados slave, had been practicing witchcraft with the girls, but more important, the best minds of the time, here and in Europe, inside and outside the churches, would have been indignant to be told there were no witches when the Bible on three different occasions warns against dealing with them.[16]

Second, the motivation of chief accuser Abigail Williams was to get rid of John Proctor's wife Elizabeth. Miller reports how he found evidence of

> the breakdown of the Proctor marriage and Abigail Williams's determination to get Elizabeth murdered so that she could have John, whom I deduced she had slept with while she was their house servant, before Elizabeth fired her.[17]

Conflicts over Inheritance

Besides authentic sorcery and sexual plotting, economic factors in Massachusetts apparently entered the cauldron of motives for the Salem trials.

In her study of witchcraft in Colonial New England, Carol F. Karlsen theorizes that many women accused of witchcraft posed a more mundane threat: they stood to inherit property which would ordinarily have gone to a male. Overcrowding in New England communities was causing inheritance problems and escalating boundary disputes. Karlsen describes how land disputes and social conflicts often preceded accusations of witchcraft.

> We know that most witches . . . were inheriting or potentially inheriting women. We know too what distinguishes these women from other

women in similar economic positions and what unites them with other accused witches: the community's view of them as discontented, angry, envious, malicious, seductive, lying, and proud women. Most witches did express dissatisfaction, however indirectly, with the power arrangements of their society, and in doing so they raised the specter of witchcraft, of female rebellion against God and man.[18]

There is evidence that the Puritan view of the man as the head of the household was threatened by the prospect of women inheriting land, especially when a man's own sons were going to suffer because of the meager resources he had to leave them.

Freedom from Religion

There is another side to the condemnation of terrible things done in the name of Christianity. Terrible things have also been done in the name of freedom from religion.

An example from near the time of our own American Revolution is the French Revolution, which was founded on the ideas of the Enlightenment *philosophes* who enthroned human reason as ultimate. They often disagreed with one another, writes historian Peter Grey, but the one thing this "impressive clan of radical intellectuals" had in common was "a critical attitude toward any sort of orthodoxy, and especially towards orthodox religion."[19] In the new French "Republic of Virtue," "Christianity was equated with counterrevolution, and a program of de-Christianization raised the 'Cult of Reason' in its place."[20]

Maximilien Robespierre, main leader and champion of the "Committee of Public Safety," was a disciple of Jean-Jacques Rousseau, for whom human civilization was the chief problem of humanity. Freedom was to be found in a return to primitive society.

Theoretically this individual freedom would be perfectly reflected in the "general will" through the social contract. The utopianism of this concept was shown by the French Revolution's Reign of Terror, during which the purification of the general will meant not only the loss of freedom for the individual but the reign of the guillotine.[21]

In May 1794 Robespierre revolutionized the French calendar and substituted new holidays for the old Christian ones. He "proposed an entire cycle of revolutionary festivals, to begin with the Festival of the Supreme Being," which was "intended to celebrate a new civil religion as opposed to Christianity as it was to the atheism of the extreme dechristianizers."[22] At the June 8 festival, a combined celebration of nature worship and military power, Robespierre addressed the crowds:

> The eternally happy day which the French people consecrates to the Supreme Being has finally arrived. . . . Did not his immortal hand, by engraving in the hearts of men the code of justice and equality, write there the death sentence of tyrants? . . . . The Author of Nature linked all mortals together in an immense chain of love and happiness. Perish the tyrants who have dared to break it![23]

Robespierre's threat came back on his own head. "Two days after the Festival of the Supreme Being, the Terror was intensified by the passage of a new law expanding the definition of suspected persons and relaxing the rules of evidence for the Revolutionary Tribunal."[24] Robespierre himself was overthrown and executed in July.

The French revolutionaries were certain that they were bringing in a new order with humanity reigning supreme. "As in the later Russian Revolution," wrote Francis Schaeffer, "the revolutionaries on their humanist base had only two options—anarchy or repression."[25]

Communism: Official Atheism

Not long after the collapse of the Soviet Union, which had been an atheistic regime actively suppressing Christianity, we spent a year in Kharkov, Ukraine. The Orthodox Church was tolerated under Communism, but many of its beautiful buildings fell into disrepair. Now all over the city we saw Orthodox churches being restored.

Under Communism one magnificent church had been turned into a concert hall, the altar displaced by organ console and pipes. When we attended a concert there, religious icons were being displayed on the walls again. Two blocks from our apartment there was a wreck of a church; we visited its grounds often because it had a spring where we got our drinking water. Week by week we watched the church glow with new life as it was renovated inside and out.

In Kharkov the non-Orthodox Christians such as Baptists and Pentecostals had no beautiful buildings to restore, but they were building connections with Western Christians and seeking Bible study materials in Russian. Visiting mission groups were holding Christian festivals and planting fellowship groups in the city. Christians relished the new air of freedom as the country came out from under seven decades of censorship.

Marxism, the basis of Communism, had no choice but to suppress Christianity and all other religions. As a strictly materialistic view of the world, Marxism has no room for spiritual realities. Karl Marx adopted the German philosopher Hegel's concept of history as "dialectic process." All aspects of human history, Hegel said, inevitably go through a three-step cycle of thesis, antithesis and synthesis. In the 1848 *Communist Manifesto,* Marx and Friedrich Engels wrote that this inevitable process would consume religion along with everything else:

> When the ancient world was in its last throes, the ancient religions were overcome by Christianity. When Christian ideas succumbed in the eighteenth century to rationalist ideas, feudal society fought its death-battle with the then revolutionary bourgeoisie. The ideas of religious liberty and freedom of conscience merely gave expression to the sway of free competition within the domain of knowledge.[26]

The Communist revolution is the most radical rupture with traditional property relations; no wonder that its development involves the most radical rupture with traditional ideas.

Unburdened by traditionally held truths, Communists were free to ignore history and shape the new world in their own image. Along the way, the leadership had to deal with those who didn't share their vision of how society should be organized.

At the state university in Ukraine where we taught English, our students told us they were just finding out about Stalin's starvation and deportation of Ukrainian farmers in the 1930s. That part of their history, they told us, was a "white" or blank period which had been kept from them. The Ukrainian farmers were not some enemy force but were Stalin's own Soviet citizens whose only crime was resisting his efforts to collectivize. Devoid of any moral basis, Communism had only repression to bring the peasants to their knees.

Nazism: Pseudo-Christianity

Nazism took a more devious approach to Christianity, using the church rather than outlawing it. Adolph Hitler's strategy was to co-opt the church and manipulate it for his own purposes by enlisting it as a patriotic force for National Socialism.

Nazism was built on Friedrich Nietzsche's concept of the "overman." Nietzsche himself "regarded traditional Christian morality as a 'slave morality,' incompatible with the great life struggle, the aim of which should be to produce a new race of supermen."[27]

The basic tenet of Nazi ideology was belief in the moral supremacy of the Aryan race, whom the Nazis identified with the Teutonic ancestors of the German Volk. According to Hitler, the whole of history was a cosmic struggle by this "master race" to dominate various "inferior" races, such as the Slavs, the Latins, and especially the Jews. . . .

The Nazi notion of a "master race" fitted well with Nietzsche's concept of a "superman" who was not bound by ordinary conventions of law and morality. So, too, did their emphasis on eternal struggle, violence, and power for its own sake.[28]

Not all German Christians concurred with Hitler's misuse of the church, and many paid the ultimate price for their resistance. In the Barmen Declaration of 1934, dissenters such as Dietrich Bonhoeffer pledged their loyalty to Christ above the German state. The declaration ended with these words:

We repudiate the false teaching that the church, in human self-esteem, can put the word and work of the Lord in the service of some wishes, purposes and plans or other, chosen according to desire. The Word of God lasts forever. Amen.[29]

The Nazis understood very well that true Christianity was antithetical to their cause. They denounced members of the dissident Confessing Church, and many—including Bonhoeffer—they executed.

Modern Martyrs

Religious researchers believe there have been more Christian martyrs in the twentieth century than in any other. David Neff reports that "the typical Christian lives in a developing country, speaks a non-European language, and exists under the constant threat of persecution—of murder, imprisonment, torture, or rape."[30]

Michael Horowitz received Prison Fellowship's 1997 William Wilberforce Award for "exemplary perseverance and selflessness in combatting injustice." Horowitz, who is Jewish, is Senior Fellow of the Hudson Institute, a private, not-for-profit research organization founded in 1961. In an interview with Charles Colson, Horowitz had this to say about modern religious persecution:

> I see eerie parallels between the way the elites of the world are dealing with Christians (who have become the scapegoats of choice for the thug regimes around the world) and the way the elites dealt with the Jews when Hitler came to power. . . .
>
> Friedrich Nietzsche made a chilling prediction near the beginning of the twentieth century. He said that God was going to die in the eyes of enlightened man, but that there would be another god—politics— and this god would be a lot more bloody, a lot more efficient, and that the sins committed in the name of politics would dwarf by orders of magnitude all the sins committed in the name of religion.[31]

A Salve That Goes Deeper

Does any of this adequately answer the accusation that "Christians have done terrible things in the name of Christ"? It may be of some help. In defense of authentic Christianity, we can repudiate the paranoia of the Salem witch trials and we can point out evils done by anti-Christian regimes.

But when the terrible things have been done to us personally, when we have been profoundly hurt in a church, we want a salve that goes deeper than historic fact. We want an answer that goes all the way down to our souls. Our hearts demand justice. How can these things happen? How can even the best and most respectable Christians deal out such pain to others—both inside and outside their ranks—and not even feel remorse about it?

There's a clue in something said by a hero of the 1991 Gulf War, General Norman Schwarzkopf. After the U.S. victory, Schwarzkopf complained about his surprising new lack of personal power. "Seven months ago I could give a single command and 541,000 people would immediately obey it," he grumbled. "Today I can't get a plumber to come to my house."[32]

It's comforting to know that even General Schwarzkopf can feel powerless. Most of us hate the feeling of being out of control. We like personal power. We might claim we only want to control our own destinies, but in order to control our own destinies we usually need to control other people too—whether plumbers, soldiers or church council members.

The Drive for Power

We humans come equipped with a complex of inner drives. God graciously provides legitimate channels for most of our drives to be expressed and fulfilled—hunger, thirst, sex, creativity, security, relationship. Though in an imperfect world not everyone gets every drive satisfied, still the moral channels do exist.

But it seems we have one drive for which God provides no safe channel for expression and release, and that is our drive for power. This drive is the one that has to be given up if we are going to live in the right relationship with each other and with our Creator.

Most pain in churches happens because people's personal power drives run into each other. When we have strong ideas about how things should go, but we aren't submitting fully to the Spirit of Christ and aren't trusting him to make things happen in his own time, then we have to resort to trying to control each other. Whether the conflict is superficially polite or openly cruel, the issue is still control.

The power struggle shouldn't happen, but it does, and the church which claims to be immune is kidding itself or naive. When Scripture says, "All have sinned and fall short of the glory of God" (Rom 3:23), the diagnosis includes every Christian. Sin flows as easily through religious channels as through secular channels. In fact religion gives our power drive the added bonus of a sense of self-righteousness.

Inconsistent with Christ

The atheists' home page has every right to accuse certain Christians of shockingly unchristian actions and attitudes. But that is just the point: they are *un*christian actions and attitudes. When Christians act from the drive for power, we are not acting in line with true Christianity; we are acting inconsistently with the faith we claim.

Christ's disciples got into an argument about who would be the greatest in the kingdom of God. They weren't fighting on behalf of each other's honor but were trying to secure their own status in the coming kingdom. Jesus quickly reminded them that the nature of his kingdom was not power but service.

Jesus called them together and said, "You know that those who are regarded as rulers of the Gentiles lord it over them, and their high officials exercise authority over them. Not so with you. Instead, whoever wants to become great among you must be your servant, and whoever wants to be first must be slave of all. For even the Son of Man did not come to be served, but to serve, and to give his life as a ransom for many." (Mk 10:42-45)

When the church acts out of the drive for power, lording it over its own members or crushing the opposition, it acts inconsistently with its own teachings about service and self-surrender. Actions like that are not a true picture of the nature of Christianity. On the other hand, when Hitler and Stalin ordered the deaths of their own fellow citizens, they were acting consistently with their own philosophy of life as a relentless power struggle.

Who Will Be God?

As Richard Thompson and a fellow seminary student were debating the long-standing theological question of free will and the sovereignty of God, Thompson realized that he did not really want God to be God—not "God" in the sense of the One who deserves submission and obedience in every area of life. Suddenly the discussion moved out of the theoretical. The young seminarian faced a practical and troubling question: who would be the master of his life—himself or God? "Was he Lord or was

I? Did I know God as that intensely personal Creator of the universe fully revealed in Christ? And more importantly, did I want to?"

Years later, researching new religious movements for the Spiritual Counterfeits Project in Berkeley, California, Thompson saw religious cults promising the godlike power which people crave. He also realized again that, no matter how good a Christian he thought he was, he had that same power drive in his own heart. "That tremendous will to power resides in us all. If honest, we will admit our desire for absolute control—if not of the universe, then at least of our own lives. It is the age-old problem of wanting to be God."

For Richard Thompson the answer was grace—God's unearned and undeserved acceptance in Christ. But first he had to face his own drive to be his own God.

> I found myself clenching my fists as I realized that I was there 2,000 years ago with the crowd before Pilate shouting, "Crucify him!" I could not stand the light of Christ's holiness. I hated him for revealing what was in my heart. . . . It was at that point that I experienced his grace. He had known I had felt like that all along. In fact, that kind of rebellion, that kind of hatred toward God is why he came. . . . While I was shouting, "Crucify him," he was about the business of reconciliation.[33]

Christ is still about the business of reconciliation—between God and humanity, between Christians and non-Christians, and between Christians and other Christians who have wounded each other. If you have been put off by the hurtful actions of Christians, know that God's grace reaches out to you and, through you, can even reach out to them.

6/ "Christian Missionaries Destroy Native Cultures"

MYTH #6: "Christian missionaries force indigenous peoples to give up their unique culture. Christians don't respect the spiritual value in native customs and religions."

"Dr. Livingstone, I presume."
—New York Herald reporter Henry Stanley, on finding missionary David Livingstone, who had disappeared into the African jungle seven years earlier; at Ujiji, Africa, 1871

In 1853, Catholic missionaries from Mission Santa Barbara in California sailed to San Nicolas, an island seventy miles off the coast, and persuaded the small band of native residents there to return with them to the mission. The endeavor ended in tragedy for the natives.

After their boat put off from the island, it was discovered that a baby had been left behind. The captain refused to turn back, claiming that the landing would be too difficult. The baby's distraught mother jumped overboard and was last seen swimming toward the rocky shore. It was assumed that she died in the rough surf.

Within a few years, all of the San Nicolas Indians brought to the mission had died. Eighteen years later, seal hunters thought they spotted a lone woman on San Nicolas. A search party was sent out. They found the woman. Her child had died, and she was the sole survivor of her people. They brought her back to the mainland. Within a few months she too died, never having communicated with anyone.[1]

Missionary Meddlers

Just as in a hologram where every part contains the whole, the San Nicolas tragedy carries the full stereotype of how Christian missionaries trample on indigenous cultures. Here's how the story goes:

The missionaries arrive uninvited. Despite noble intentions, they are ignorant of the place where they set up shop and indifferent to the hearts and values of the people they have come to help. They meddle in things which are none of their business. They assume that the natives' traditional spirituality is defective, even devilish. They bribe or coerce the people to abandon their traditional ways until, in the process of trying to "save" the people, the missionaries wind up destroying them.

In his beautifully illustrated *Endangered Peoples,* written for the 1993 Year of the World's Indigenous Peoples, Art Davidson expounds the popular view that in the process of religious "conversion" everyone loses. The natives lose their spiritual heritage; Westerners lose because indigenous peoples drink from a well of spirituality which Westerners have not tasted.

While technological people value saving and acquiring, indigenous people value sharing and giving. In Western cultures, spirituality is usually separated from the rest of life; in native cultures it is integrated with daily living. Technological societies tend to adopt the concept of a single, paternalistically defined God or else incline toward atheism.[2]

Life-and-Death Devotion

Today there are ethnologists, photographers and oral historians working to preserve traditional cultures and educate the rest of the world about them. Their commitment to indigenous peoples sends them to the remotest places—what pioneering missionaries called "the ends of the earth."

Few of these people, however, start to approach the life-and-death devotion of the pioneer missionary so often blamed for trampling on foreign cultures.

Haunted by the vision that "every day tens of thousands were passing away to Christless graves!"[3], Europeans and Americans left comfortable homes and families in the great missionary movement of the nineteenth century. They traveled to little-known places where communication with the outside world was sparse or nonexistent. They stayed there not for a few weeks of investigation, but to live and probably to die there.

The beginnings of the modern missions movement in the Protestant churches are usually traced to William Carey, a young English pastor and shoemaker. In the late 1700s he was gripped by the conviction—unpopular in his circles at the time—that Christians needed to go out and aggressively take the gospel to all nations of the world. In his 1792 "Enquiry into the Obligation of Christians to Use Means for the Conversion of the Heathens," Carey answered several objections to foreign missions, including the possibility of death at the hands of the natives:

> In respect to the danger of being killed by them, it is true that whoever does go must put his life in his hand, and not consult with flesh and blood; but do not the goodness of the cause, the duties incumbent on us as the creatures of God, and Christians, and the perishing state of our fellow men, loudly call upon us to venture all and use every warrantable exertion for their benefit?[4]

Compelled by such devotion, Christian missionaries never set out to destroy people but to save them temporally and eternally. Then how did the tragedies of destruction happen?

A Cultural Marathon

Recently we talked with two linguistic missionaries on furlough from their work in a remote part of the world. They describe the society in which they are living, working and raising their children as "a traditional nonindustrial people in transition." It has been an oral society with no written language. They have given years—and expect to give more years—putting the native language into writing and teaching the people to read their own language.

The two missionaries raise this interesting point: as indigenous peoples must be understood culturally, the missionary of the past must be understood culturally also. "Earlier missionaries were influenced by evolutionary ideas," they told us. "They believed that people were supposed to progress from hunters to hunter-gatherers to farmers, then to having industry."

According to Don Richardson, an influential contemporary missionary who has lived with some of the world's most "primitive" peoples, the dominant picture of human society in the nineteenth century was a worldwide foot race from stone age to technological age.

> Nineteenth-century theories of biological and cultural evolution strongly implied the probability that one branch of mankind, the European branch, had already outdistanced the rest of mankind in physical and cultural evolution. . . . Picture all human societies as runners in a gigantic cultural "marathon." The goal is to race from the cultural simplicity of the stone age toward the ultimate cultural achievement of an ideal society enjoying technological mastery over nature.[5]

Christianizing = Civilizing

As we saw in chapter four, the evolutionary view of humanity was embraced by many nineteenth-century clergy as a guarantee of progress. Missionaries of that era carried with them not only the promises of God but the optimism of their own times. They urgently wanted to spread the news of salvation in Jesus, which they believed would make the eternal difference between heaven and hell. Meanwhile, this side of heaven, they wanted to raise the savage and the pagan from barbarian darkness to enlightened civilization.

Paul Johnson, who spends 1,000 pages analyzing how the world changed in the fifteen years between 1815 and 1830, explains how for missionaries of that time Christianity and civilization were inseparable:

> It was a constant theme of missionary literature, 1815-30, that backward races were the victims of their environment . . . and that knowledge of Christianity could raise them, sooner rather than later, to the level of whites. The constitution of the Aborigines Protection Society laid down that "the complete Civilisation and the real Happiness of

Man can never be secured by anything less than the diffusion of Christian principles."[6]

Missions historian R. Pierce Beaver shows how universal was the "civilizing" theme in missions:

> Even in countries with a high culture, such as India and China, European missionaries stressed the "civilizing" objective as much as their brethren in primitive regions because they regarded the local culture as degenerate and superstitious—a barrier to christianization. During the early decades there was never debate about the legitimacy of the stress on the civilizing function of missions. Debate was only about priority; which came first, christianization or civilization?[7]

Cultural Imperialism?

The issues get confused when the Christian missionary movement is equated with general European and American expansionism and put under the heading of "imperialism." Steven J. Keillor, a historian himself, points out that "historians often use imperialism to mean little more than Americans going to new places to trade or preach. . . . Historians have stretched imperialism to cover cases where non-Western peoples preferred Western goods, religion or culture."[8] Keillor explains how secular historians often doom missionaries to a no-win situation:

> Historians place missionaries in impossible dilemmas. They are often condemned no matter what they do. If they offer practical assistance, they are changing the culture. If they just preach the gospel, they are ignoring human needs. If they teach in English, they are altering the culture. If they teach in the native language, they are denying people the advantage of a command of English. The historian creates an artificial dichotomy between helping people and saving souls.[9]

It's undeniable that Western expansionists in general exploited and demolished indigenous cultures. Outsiders who are driven only by the profit motive will naturally have less concern for the native people than will outsiders who see the natives as God's creations with eternal souls worth saving. As European-owned tea, coffee and sugar plantations expanded through Africa, India and the Americas, great numbers of native peoples

were displaced or pressed into service on the plantations. The interconti-
nental slave trade developed to supply cheap workers for the sugar and
cotton plantations in the Americas.

Some missionaries saw the growing tragedy and looked for practical
economic solutions. The most famous early missionary to Africa was
David Livingstone, born in Scotland, who sailed for Capetown in 1840.
Livingstone was a flamboyant and controversial figure, part evangelist
and part explorer. Disturbed that too many missionaries were concentrat-
ing their work on the African coast, he headed for less populated regions.
In his more than thirty years in Africa he survived a lion attack, life-threat-
ening disease and numerous safaris into territory unknown to Europeans.

The more [Livingstone] encountered the inhumane slave traffic of the
Portuguese and the Arabs, the more convinced he became that only the
combination of "Commerce and Christianity" could save Africa. He
was well aware that foreign slavers could not stay in business without
the Africans' cooperation (one tribe capturing slaves from an enemy
tribe), and his solution was to bring legitimate commerce to Africa.[10]

North American Uniqueness

While missionaries were having success in faraway lands, there was less
success back home with North American natives. Here there were unique
tensions. Only here were the natives and the culture represented by the
missionaries in direct conflict with each other about the very land on
which the mission work was happening.

Many scholars agree that Indian evangelism, as a whole, was not a
story of success, the greatest reason being the intense conflict between
the two cultures for supremacy over the land. But perhaps equally
important was the deep-seated belief of white America that Indians
were racially inferior and that their culture was not worth saving.[11]

There were notable missionary exceptions, such as with the Nez Perce
tribe. Their homeland was the Snake River Valley, where Idaho, Oregon
and Washington now meet. In 1805 the Lewis and Clark expedition
arrived there desperately needy and was befriended by the tribe.

The explorers described these Indians as a whole as a quiet, civil people, tractable in disposition, willing to be instructed, but also proud and haughty. Although the captains did not precisely say so, several entries leave the impression that the Nez Perce Indians were their favorites.[12]

In 1836 missionaries Henry and Elisa Spalding (or Spaulding) arrived and were welcomed by the Nez Perce. They could see the imminent danger to the Indians' mobile economy of food-gathering, hunting, fishing and breeding large herds of horses and cattle. A secular history spells out their efforts to help the Nez Perce survive:

> Spalding recognized that the Christian purpose would be achieved best if settled community life could be developed. He also realized that white expansion would raise havoc with the old bison-hunting and salmon-fishing economy. If the Nez Perces were to become Christian farmers their chance for survival was good. To that end he served as both pastor and foreman, and in both roles his bearing was austere. He and his wife Elisa labored with great zeal, and the fact that the Nez Perce Christians became the most advanced Indians in the arts of civilized life is due to the Spaldings.[13]

In 1860, when gold was discovered on the Nez Perce land, the tribe's future was tragically sealed. Some of the tribe signed a treaty with the United States government in 1863; others refused. After violent conflicts in the 1870s, Chief Joseph surrendered. The Nez Perce were moved down the Yellowstone and Missouri Rivers to the Oklahoma Territory, where many soon died. "The Indian Rights Association and the Presbyterian Church both recommended the return of the Nez Perces to a mountain environment,"[14] and eventually some did return, but their numbers had been decimated.

The Snowshoe Priest

For several months in 1997, Duluth's historical society presented an unusual exhibit called "Shared Horizons." The exhibit celebrated both the 200th birthday of Catholic missionary Father Frederic Baraga and the native American culture where "the snowshoe priest" immersed thirty years of his life.

Father Baraga immigrated to the United States from Slovenia in 1830 to serve the Diocese of Cincinnati, which took in present-day Ohio, Michigan and Wisconsin. He was increasingly drawn to the Lake Superior region. Working at first through an interpreter, Father Baraga studied the Ottawa language and gradually compiled an Ottawa dictionary and prayer book. Later he did the same for the similar Ojibwe language.

Father Baraga saw how the Indians' feast-or-famine nomadic life of hunting and gathering opened them up to exploitation by white fur traders. He encouraged his converts to learn agriculture and store food to survive the winters. The priest's life was threatened when white traders learned that Catholic Indian converts were unwilling to barter furs for whiskey. He faced more opposition from white traders and government agents than from native Americans.

Father Baraga's first chapels were built of birch bark. He learned to snowshoe and for the next decades traveled throughout the Lake Superior region teaching Christianity and doing all he could to provide clothing, medicine, farming tools and education for the Ojibwe.[15] Baraga's pioneering Ojibwe grammar and dictionary are still in print and in use today. The priest's willingness to become fluent in the language of his parishioners was key to his fruitfulness, as Bernard J. Lambert says it was key to the relative success of Catholic over Protestant missions to native Americans:

> The children attending Protestant schools in other portions of the Indian country were taught in English, which could be understood only by the whites and not by their Indian brethren. Catholic teachers firmly believed that if an Indian was taught in his own language the education would be of greater practical use to him. . . . This system added greater burdens to the life of a missionary, but it was easier for one man to learn the Ottawa tongue than for a whole nation to learn English.[16]

A Passion for Language

If a missionary or anyone else wanted to kill a culture, killing the language would certainly be the way to do it. When a culture loses its language, it loses its soul.

Linguists now predict that fewer than half the world's six thousand languages will survive our children's generation. In the coming century, 90 percent of humankind's languages are likely to disappear. . . . In North America, for example, fifty-one languages have become extinct in just the last thirty years. But who can name even one of them? Who knows who these people were?[17]

Christianity is a word-oriented religion. The written word (Scripture) and the spoken word (preaching and teaching) are vital to Christian faith. Since the Protestant Reformation, the dominant view has been that religious texts and rituals should be in the language of the common people. For linguistic missionaries, such as the two we met, the native language becomes their consuming interest and life's work.

To a lay person the linguistic missionary's job sounds too difficult to believe, let alone attempt. If the Bible is going to be introduced to a culture, it must be translated into the language of that culture, which may have no equivalents for biblical concepts such as the Good Shepherd or crucifixion or even forgiveness by the supreme God. If the culture is purely oral and has no written language, the missionary must first do what Father Baraga did—*invent* an orthography, devising symbols and putting the language into writing for the first time. Missionaries are so closely identified with putting languages into writing that our 1989 *Webster's Unabridged Dictionary* illustrates the word "orthography" with the sentence "Missionaries provided the first orthography for the language"![18]

Liberating Literacy

In giving the people the Bible in written form, the missionary also gives them the earth-shaking power of literacy. That's dangerous. If the indigenous people can read the Bible, they can also read anything else that comes along, whether compatible with Christianity or not.

Giving a people the gift of literacy is the opposite of compelling them to submit to an imperialistic culture. Literacy is liberating, and therefore it is risky. The linguistic missionary gladly takes that risk. The two we met explain how their work preserves rather than destroys the language of the people:

If they can get their language in writing, they will never lose it. We call this "mother-tongue literacy." We take their native language, put it into writing and teach people to read and write their own language.

In the past, their folklore was passed on by storytellers. But now parents would be angry if the kids spent their time at the storyteller's house, because the kids should be home studying their schoolwork. To have some of these stories in print and distributed is not taking something away from the people, but giving it back to them.

Going Native

While some nineteenth-century missionaries assumed that conversion to Christianity meant having to adopt Western ways, there was increasing momentum to adopt native dress and lifestyle where it did not conflict with Christian convictions or morality.

In the 1850s the English physician James Hudson Taylor was working in Shanghai under the Chinese Evangelization Society. Put off by what he considered the luxurious living style of other missionaries, he began to consider adopting Chinese dress and perhaps taking to a boat for his living quarters. His son and daughter-in-law explained how radical this step would be:

> Wearing Chinese dress in those days involved shaving the front part of the head and letting the hair grow long for the regulation queue. No missionary or other foreigner conformed to such a custom. For an occasional journey, a Chinese gown might be used over one's ordinary clothing, but to give up European dress and adopt the native costume altogether was quite another matter.[19]

On a solitary 200-mile evangelistic journey up the Yangtze River, Taylor found that his fair-haired, blue-eyed northern European appearance got in the way.

> Attention was continually distracted from his message by his appearance, which to his hearers was as undignified as it was comical. And after all, surely it mattered more to be suitably attired from the Chinese point of view—when it was the Chinese he wanted to win—rather than sacrifice their approval for that of the small foreign community in the Ports.[20]

When the missionary couple with whom he worked departed for the interior of China, Taylor was left alone in Shanghai, his living quarters usurped by other Englishmen. Then he was unexpectedly offered a Chinese-style house in the southern part of the city, away from foreigners. "He accepted it, and resolved henceforth to wear native dress and live upon Chinese food."[21]

That night he took the step which was to have so great an influence on the evangelization of inland China! When the barber had done his best, the young missionary darkened his remaining hair to match the long black braid which, at first, must do duty for his own. Then in the morning he put on as best he might the loose, unaccustomed garments, and appeared for the first time in the gown and satin shoes of the "Teacher," or man of the scholarly class.

Everything opened up after that in a new way. . . . While missing some of the prestige attaching to Europeans, he found it more than made up for by the freedom his changed appearance gave him in moving among the people.[22]

Taylor's new appearance caused some consternation among his fellow missionaries and his own family back home, writes missions historian Ruth Tucker, "but if Taylor had second thoughts about his decision, he never made them known, and his adoption of Chinese dress and culture became his trademark."[23]

The linguistic missionaries working in a closed culture tell us, "Almost all the missionaries in our generation have been raised on Hudson Taylor's model, not the earlier model."

Real Natives

Taylor and the China Inland Mission he founded in 1865 had a profound influence on Christian students in England. Seven of Britain's best and brightest young men, who had distinguished themselves in cricket, rowing or the military, gave themselves to Taylor's mission and sailed for China. There they immediately adopted Chinese dress and living style.

One of these "Cambridge Seven," C. T. Studd, was also deeply affected by a letter from Booth Tucker of the Salvation Army in India, which he took for an example and a challenge:

Our party have no salaries, get no money, and having food and raiment, they learn to be therewith content. No grumbling or arguing is heard in our camp. Both lads and lassies go bare foot (for preference). For meals they have rice water in the morning, rice and vegetable curries (no meat) at midday and the same in the evening. The use of tea and coffee is quite given up as being too European! The floor of the quarters being well raised and dug, we have abolished beds. There are no chairs and tables in the camp. I am myself sitting squatted on a mat, with my papers round me on the floor. Nevertheless we really are very comfortable and as happy as possible. . . . We have constant victory and God is showing us how to manage and train these officers and manufacture them into real natives.[24]

It would be deceptive to leave the impression that pioneer missionaries adopted indigenous customs as their stamp of approval on the equal value of all cultures. They did it to open channels of connection and communication because they had something life-changing, even life-saving, to give to the indigenous people. They altered their appearance and living styles not for the sake of cultural diversity but for the sake of the gospel.

Traditions That Conflict

One of the first things that appalled William Carey when he went to India as a pioneer missionary was the practice of *suttee,* the burning of widows alive on the funeral pyres of their deceased husbands. Through the efforts of Christian missionaries *suttee* has been officially abolished in India. Few Westerners would say that the culture-changing influence of Christianity was harmful there.

But what about other practices which Western Christians—and for that matter, Westerners in general—would find repugnant? What does a missionary do with traditions such as the headhunting of the seminomadic Punan in Borneo?

[U]nlike some other headhunting tribes, [the Punan] do not massacre wantonly. They cut heads only for ritual reasons . . . or to serve in some important ceremony . . . but especially for weddings. . . . The prospect of marriage brings with it a serious problem. A woman cannot marry until she has found a soul. Her future husband must procure one for her. He sets off on a headhunt. When he returns with his treasure, a lengthy ceremony ensues for the transmission of the soul. . . . [The shaman] determines whether or not the transmutation has been successful. If not, another head must be sought and the entire ceremony repeated.[25]

Or what about the traditional wife-trading rite of *papisj* among the Asmat people in Irian Jaya, New Guinea?

The *papisj* is a marital exchange between two couples. The men agree on the conditions; their wives must be consulted, however, and must consent. On rare occasions, there are also community *papisj*, involving all of the clans of the village. Some ethnologists view this practice as a means of seeking revenge on an unfriendly environment or of exorcising misfortune and death. It is as if man, by an excessive display of sexuality, could compensate for the high death rate by creating mass births.[26]

Modern missionaries would not require the Punan to give up their nomadic lifestyle or their hunting. But is the headhunting necessary to preserve their cultural identity? When the Bible teaches that each individual has a soul given by God, should a woman without a husband be encouraged to regard herself as soulless? Should she be regarded as soulless by the men of the tribe until another man is murdered for her? Given the Christian view of the sacredness of the marriage bond, could Christian Asmat in good conscience continue to trade marital partners?

The nonjudgmental ethnologist would say, "Don't interfere. If you were really open-minded, you'd understand the reasons why they do these things you find so repugnant, and anyway, who are you to judge?" What business do missionaries have "civilizing" anybody? Who are they to say that a culture needs to revise its spirituality and change its religion and customs?

Searching for a *Beleyola*

In refreshing contrast to the stereotype of the missionary imposing change, change sometimes originates not with the missionary but with the native Christian. Paul Noren, the missionary whom we met in chapter three, tells of a recent incident in the country where he was born:

A Zairian Christian was building a new cattle pen, and his uncle insisted that they follow tradition and cut a particular tree (a *beleyola*), put it into the middle of the pen and dedicate the place to the ancestor spirits. The ceremony was against the beliefs of the Christian, but he wanted to respect his elder. The uncle went out and searched all day but could not find any *beleyola*, though he knew they grew everywhere. Meanwhile the Christian was asking himself, "Should we be doing this? Should I be letting my uncle do this? I don't believe in the spirits."

When the uncle came back with no tree, the Christian announced that they would go ahead and dedicate the cattle pen—but they would dedicate it to Jesus Christ instead of to the ancestor spirits. The family gathered around and prayed. After the dedication to Christ, when they went to cut poles for fencing, they saw *beleyola* after *beleyola*, including some right at the place where they hung their clothes while they bathed.

The Zairian Christian had no question that the Lord had protected him. The power of the true God had kept him from being distracted by the influence of the spirits.

That incident from the 1990s shows a native Christian deciding how to incorporate his faith with the "old ways." The two linguistic missionaries tell us how they operate in a way which encourages nationals to find their own balance between tradition and the newness of the gospel:

We are no longer dictating to people what parts of their culture to throw away or keep. We're letting the Bible do that. We say, let God change the aspects of the culture which are not godly.

We find a lot of spiritual value in the traditions of the people we work with. The new converts have a good idea about what belongs and what they need to break from. But they don't know everything they need to throw off at once. That comes through Bible study. And they'll ask us—we don't totally keep silent.

The change to be made comes out of *relationship*. I ask, "What do you think God wants you to do?" Or I point to something in the Bible about a similar situation. These questions have to come *from* the new converts. We're not wise enough to know what needs to be addressed. We might be addressing something unimportant when something very important is lacking.

Where Helping Ends and Meddling Begins

Some argue that the best change for traditional cultures is no change at all. But is that either possible or desirable? Should Westerners withhold medical advances, well-drilling technology or modern communications and leave people in the Stone Age? Changes brought by Christian missionaries at least come with the moderating ethic of concern for people as creations of God.

Ironically, many secular Westerners think nothing of jumping in and encouraging change in indigenous cultures when change would benefit Westerners.

With population growth slowing in developed countries, Westerners are strongly pushing birth control in the parts of the world where population growth is still explosive. The effort furthers two values very important in the West: improved status and freedom for women, and the lessening of population pressure so there is more to go around for all of us (especially for those of us in the West). But in societies where the survival of the clan depends on having a large family and where parents need numerous children to care for them in their old age, successfully "pushing" birth control radically changes the traditional culture.

Photographers Carol Beckwith and Angela Fisher have worked for twenty-five years documenting traditional African ceremonies. In the process of exposing the outside world to previously hidden rituals, they do the reverse as well and expose traditional peoples to the outside world.

[The] photographers have gone out of their way to repay indigenous Africans for the access they've been granted. They have, for example, established a Maasai primary school, helped Africans get educated in the West, purchased medicine and even helped dig wells. But it isn't always easy, says Fisher, to decide where helping ends and meddling begins. "It's a real conflict for us," she says. "Should we be exposing these groups to the outside world or should we leave them alone?"[27]

The question of whether traditional indigenous peoples should be kept pure may already be pointless as isolation has become impossible. In the opinion of Ralph Winter and David Fraser:

It is impossible to keep tribal peoples isolated and "safe" from modern society. For good and mostly for bad, the tribal groups are being transformed. Where the faith of Jesus Christ has been potent, it has eased the impact of the modern world. Missionaries have been among the most ardent defenders of the rights and dignity of the tribals. Their voices have been heard against multi-national corporation land seizures and governmental neglect. . . . Where whole tribes have become Christian, economic and educational uplift has been enormous. But new problems of survival and finding a place in the modern world system put even greater demands on mission agencies ill-equipped to deal with such issues.[28]

One of the linguistic missionaries we met put it in more down-to-earth terms:

In our village there are a dozen little hotels, and half of them have satellite dishes, and men are sitting inside looking at Oprah and Phil. No missionary did that. That was done by Ted Turner.

These people are changing whether they want to change or not. Most missionaries who have their heads on straight are trying to help them not change too fast, because they don't know what they're doing to themselves.

A Seed in Many Soils

Today's missionaries are "more careful than ever to avoid any tactics that would associate them with Western imperialism. They are more likely than ever to seek to preserve colorful cultural traditions that were once viewed as unchristian."[29] The challenge to any missionary is still to preach the pure gospel and then allow those who hear and follow to adapt the gospel to their own culture. "As Mr. Murthi, an Indian evangelist, put it, 'Do not bring us the Gospel as a potted plant. Bring us the seed of the Gospel and plant it in our soil.'"[30]

Paul Noren describes the changes in mission strategy he experienced while growing up in Zaire:

When we were little kids, there were rules that white people couldn't eat with black people. This wasn't mission law, it was pre-1960 Belgian law, before independence. But how do you keep little kids from eating with their African friends? Our parents started defying the rules. Just before independence, one of the African pastors invited the white missionaries to a feast. Some people were afraid to go. It was the first time the blacks and whites had ever eaten together.

In the late sixties when my dad went out on evangelistic trips, he would take his own food and water. The Africans were still afraid to feed the missionaries. Starting about 1972 or 1973, the Africans began to say, "If you come to our village, you're our guest and we're going to feed you."

[In 1997] there are still barriers coming down. Missionaries and Africans are becoming more aware of each other's cultural tendencies. Missionaries are always emphasizing financial efficiency and technological competence, while the Africans are often more worried about relationships. Both groups are realizing that they need to work at understanding each other better and that there is mutual benefit in doing so.

Heathen in Need of Salvation?

Some churches in the United States are experiencing such self-doubt about their own religious imperialism, especially toward native Americans, that they have taken the remarkable step of repudiating their own missionary efforts. While any church or mission organization might admit to specific instances of pushing Western culture, these churches' declarations are extraordinary for backpedaling even on the basic concept of converting nonbelievers to faith in Christ.

In 1987 the United Church of Christ issued a formal apology to its own native American members for the "ongoing injustice and religious imperialism" of its own missionary efforts toward them. Mentioning specific missionaries of the past by name, the UCC admitted that from its beginnings in America "mission has been understood to mean the conversion of the Indians to Christianity and to Western civilizations."

We must acknowledge that the church—our church—has, with few
exceptions, treated the Indian as a child in need of direction, as a savage
in need of civilizing, and as a heathen in need of salvation.[31]

The preceding year, the United Church of Canada had issued a similar but
shorter and more poetic apology which confessed that

In our zeal to tell you of the good news of Jesus Christ we were closed
to the value of your spirituality.

We confused Western ways and culture with the depth and breadth
and length and height of the gospel of Christ.

We imposed our civilization as a condition of accepting the gospel.[32]

Most remarkable of all, in 1987 eight Protestant denominations of the
Pacific Northwest and the Roman Catholic Archdiocese of Seattle issued
a joint apology for "long-standing participation in the destruction of
traditional Native American spiritual practices." The churches pledged
"mutual support in your efforts to reclaim and protect the legacy of your
own traditional spiritual teachings." Confessing in so many words that
Christianity had nothing to teach native Americans, the churches asked
to be taught, affirming that "the spiritual power of the land and the ancient
wisdom of your indigenous religions can be, we believe, great gifts to the
Christian church."[33]

While many Christians find such apologies too extreme, we still have
to keep facing the questions of how and whether Christianity and indigenous cultures can mix.

Redemptive Analogies

In the past twenty-five years the concept of "redemptive analogy" has
been popularized by Don Richardson (quoted earlier in this chapter
concerning the influence of evolutionary theory on missions). While the
"redemptive analogy" approach might strike unsympathetic observers as
twisting native culture to fit a Christian mold, behind it is the assumption
that God has spoken to every culture no matter how isolated it is from
Christianity. God's *general* revelation provides "redemptive analogies"
which ready the native people to receive God's *specific* revelation when
Christian messengers arrive.

The book and film *Peace Child* tell the remarkable story of how the Richardsons discovered their first "redemptive analogy." In 1962 Don and Carol and their infant son went to live with the Sawi people of New Guinea, "one of five or six tribes on the planet who practiced both cannibalism and headhunting."[34] Breaking through to the Sawi culture had its peculiar difficulties:

> Our earliest attempts to communicate the gospel to the Sawi were frustrated by their admiration of "masters of treachery"—clever deceivers who could sustain a deception of friendship over a period of months while steadily "fattening" their victims with that friendship for an unsuspected day of slaughter!
>
> Because of this unusual kind of hero-worship, the Sawi, listening to my early attempts to explain the gospel, mistook Judas Iscariot, Jesus' betrayer, for the hero of the story! Jesus, in Sawi eyes, was simply the dupe to be laughed at![35]

The Richardsons' presence attracted residents of three warring villages who normally kept out of each other's way. The tribes clashed violently until the missionaries sadly determined that, for the sake of peace, they should leave and let the people scatter again. Alarmed at the prospect of losing Carol's nursing skills and the promise of literacy, the Sawi took counsel and announced they would make peace.

It was the Sawi method of making peace that finally (in answer to prayer, the Richardsons believe) gave the "redemptive analogy" which made the gospel clear:

> If a Sawi father offered his son to another group as a "Peace Child," not only were past grievances thereby settled, but also future instances of treachery were prevented—but only as long as the Peace Child remained alive. Our ready-made key of communication, then, was the presentation of Jesus Christ to the Sawi as the ultimate Peace Child. . . .
>
> By this means, the meaning of the gospel did break through among the Sawi! Once they realized that the one Judas betrayed was a Peace Child, they no longer viewed Judas as a hero. For to betray a peace child was, to the Sawi, the worst possible crime![36]

Richardson cautions that indigenous stories should be considered "redemptive," not "redeeming." "Redeeming," he says, would mean that the people "could find relationship with God through their own lore, apart from the gospel. 'Redemptive' in this context means 'contributing to the redemption of a people, but not culminating it.'"[37]

The Peace Child analogy alone did not solve all the communication barriers to Christianity. Other analogies were also to be discovered, and for Don and Carol there were many more trying experiences to endure. But through their patient toil the Sawi gradually turned to Christianity. As a side benefit, they were also prepared to survive the inevitable "cultural disorientation" soon to be unleashed on them by the influx of oil, logging and mining industries and heavy immigration from other islands of Indonesia.[38]

We Are Going to Manage Our Own Affairs

The "cultural disorientation" faced by the Sawi is faced by all traditional peoples worldwide. Helping indigenous peoples not only survive but maintain their culture has become part of modern missionary work. This effort fails to grab the attention of those who prefer the old stereotype of missionaries, but it is happening all over the world. A few current examples:

In eastern Honduras, the Mosquitia rainforest is endangered by loggers and ranchers. "As the forest is destroyed, so is the unique lifestyle of the Indians,"[39] says Mike Webb of Tear Fund (The Evangelical Alliance Relief Fund), a Christian development agency based in England which channels practical help and workers to local Christian development efforts. The majority of La Mosquitia's 40,000 Indians are of the Miskito tribe; 80 percent of the Miskito are members of the Moravian Church, the fruit of missionary efforts begun in the 1930s. Tear Fund cooperates with MOPAWI, a Christian agency in La Mosquitia working with Indian communities toward long-range development strategy.

Health, education, training and business programmes—alongside the specific help with land rights—all aim at allowing the Indians to keep their land and to survive socially and economically.[40]

"Success," Tear Fund reported in 1997, "has included a dramatic government U-turn that prevented a big multinational corporation from logging in La Mosquitia's forests. But governments change, and many promises are yet to be kept."[41]

In chapter three we described the self-sustaining fish ponds developed by Covenant Church missionaries, first in Thailand and now in other parts of the world. The Covenant agroforestry mission in the former Zaire has promoted reforestation and the planting of fruit trees, aiming at a sustainable-yield farming system rather than one which depletes the forest resources.

In the landlocked Sahel region of Africa, YWAM (Youth With A Mission) is working to help the seminomadic Tuareg people of Niger cope with change. "In consultation with family heads and local tribal leaders, traditional well construction, agriculture, healthcare, handicrafts and literacy training are all being undertaken."

> Crucial to long-term success is the involvement of the community in the decision making process. 'No one can ignore the fact that we are brothers now,' said one Tuareg leader. 'We have woken from a long sleep, and now we are going to manage our own affairs.'[42]

In many areas missionaries help people develop their traditional crafts as salable products, making it possible for them to be self-supporting. For example, Tear Fund initiated Tearcraft, which enables indigenous peoples to market their crafts worldwide.

Ralph Winter, founder of the Pasadena research and training center called U.S. Center for World Mission, urges missionaries to honor and work within the cultures where they are called to serve:

> Jesus *died* for these people around the world. He did not die to preserve our Western way of life. He did not die to make Muslims stop praying five times a day. He did not die to make Brahmins eat meat. Can't you hear Paul the Evangelist saying we must go to these people within the systems in which they operate?[43]

Is It Love?

For evangelicals there is all the difference between recognizing the spirituality in all peoples and saying "all spiritualities are equally valid." This difference must be understood if we are going to comprehend how modern Christian missionaries resolve the tension between imposing their ideas on indigenous cultures and leaving those cultures alone. We will deal more fully with this issue in chapter seven.

Today outsiders still ask how Christians can claim to love people of all nations while daring to try to change people's religion. The answer is that Christian missionaries have always seen bringing the gospel to people as the highest expression of love—human love and God's love. Sometimes they see the fruit of their work in renewed lives and better living conditions. Sometimes they hang in for years with no reward beyond the comfort of the Holy Spirit, the acceptance of a few native people and the inner assurance that they are doing what God has called them to do.

Our own very small experience in overseas missions has put us into awkward, occasionally dangerous situations. Compared with career missionaries past and present, we have endured nothing. But we share the sharp joy of their intensely personal rewards when a student in a formerly atheistic country writes us to say, "We thank God you came to us." Our cultures met and we were both better for it. God was present in the encounter. No missionary—past, present or future—could ask for more compensation than that.

7/ "Christians Are Arrogant"

MYTH #7: "All religions teach basically the same thing, but Christians insist their religion is the only one that's right. They arrogantly claim that Jesus Christ is the only way to God. That may be true for Christians, but it isn't true for everybody."

I've given up finding the truth,
just give me a good illusion.
—saying on a tote bag carried into court by a Chicago juror

Lately when Christian friends ask us about our current writing project, we say we're working on a book about stereotypes of Christianity. We always mention that the final chapter is about how we Christians think we're the ones who have the truth. The usual response is, "Well, we *do!*"

There is neither conceit nor humor in our friends' voices when they say it. They mean it as a straightforward statement of fact. Is that arrogant? A lot of people would think so.

The Two-Stage Challenge

When Christians say we have the truth, a challenge usually gets thrown in our faces. There have been two incarnations of it. The older version has been around a long time and is fading in its frequency and sharpness. The newer version is the product of the late twentieth century; in many ways it's more slippery and harder to discuss, but it deserves a thoughtful Christian response.

The older version of the challenge is that it's arrogant of Christians to claim our religion is the right one because that's a slap in the face for other religions such as Islam, Hinduism and Buddhism. All over the world there are diverse religions, many older than Christianity, all claiming they worship the same God. Why does Christianity have to be the only path? Couldn't there be many roads up the one mountain?

The second and more contemporary version of the challenge deviates from the first in a subtle but important way. It says: "Maybe Christianity is true for you Christians, but you can't say it's true for anybody else. If somebody doesn't believe in Christianity, then for that person it isn't true. Truth is fluid. It's relative. It is within the person, not 'out there.'"

Wisdom from Humpty Dumpty

We'll deal with the second challenge first—is there such a thing as truth which is true whether or not anyone believes it? Mortimer J. Adler defined truth in a way consistent with Christian belief:

> For all who think reality exists independently of the mind and that reality is what it is regardless of how we think about it, the definition of truth is the *agreement of thought with reality*.[1]

The late Francis Schaeffer liked to call it "true truth"—that which is true regardless of whether anyone buys it or not. Does it exist? We have to deal with that question first, because if there is no such thing as truth, it's pointless to discuss which religion is true.

In *Through the Looking-Glass,* Alice meets Humpty Dumpty sitting on his wall in danger of falling. During their disjointed conversation Humpty Dumpty says "There's glory for you!" and explains that he means "There's a nice knock-down argument for you!" Alice protests that "glory" doesn't mean "a nice knock-down argument." Humpty Dumpty replies, "When I use a word, it means just what I choose it to mean—neither more nor less."[2]

"When I use a word, it means just what I choose it to mean." This time it wasn't said by Humpty Dumpty sitting on a wall but by a barefoot young woman in torn jeans and T-shirt sitting in a coffee house on Sunset Strip. It was southern California in the late sixties, and Dale was trying to have a conversation with this girl about Christianity. But they were having trouble communicating. It was getting frustrating, at least for him; she seemed to enjoy it. She insisted that it didn't matter what she believed about Christianity; she could believe it was a lie and Dale could believe it was true, and they would both be right.

The young woman's skepticism about truth went beyond religion to the basics of language. She even insisted (like Humpty Dumpty, but Dale didn't point that out) that she could use a word to mean anything she wanted it to mean. There was no final authority about the meanings of words. Finally Dale said that even if words could mean anything she chose, until the two of them agreed on the meanings, they couldn't even carry on a conversation.

Escape from the Old Rules

The barefoot woman in the coffee house was right in a way; for multitudes of young people living on the street and hitchhiking the highways, words did assume new meanings. "Love" came to mean "Spare change?"—the begging plea heard everywhere. "Free love" was reduced to physical sex without emotional relationship or mental commitment. Several of the girls who sought warmth and a sandwich in our all-night coffee house said, "We live like animals."

An earthshaking change was going on in how young Americans thought about the world. They were no longer arguing over what was true; they were saying *there was no truth to be known*. While the promises of free love eventually turned sour, the volcanic change in American thinking has persisted.

How Many Words for Snow?

Twenty years after that California conversation about words and meanings, a famous "vocabulary hoax" got shattered. It should have been a small victory for truth, but by then the idea that there is no truth was too well ingrained in North American thinking. Certain people who found the hoax useful decided to keep on believing it regardless of the facts.

The facts are these. For decades a story went around in academic circles that Eskimos have 23 words for what English speakers call "snow." Or maybe it was 17 words, or maybe 100—the story varied, and apparently nobody bothered to ask the Eskimos. Anyway, it was therefore said that Eskimo culture perceives reality differently from the way white culture perceives reality.

In 1991 anthropologist Laura Martin debunked the snow story. She showed how an initial report that Eskimos had about seven words for snow had gotten inflated through telling and retelling. Martin was "disappointed in the reaction of her colleagues when she pointed out the fallacy; most, she says, took the position that true or not, 'it's still a great example.'"[3]

A great example of what? Of something Martin's colleagues wanted to prove, perhaps, but certainly not an example of truth. Never mind. It was a 1990s reaction to a bothersome factual discovery: since nobody can say what truth is anyway, let's go on putting words (17, or 23, or maybe 100) in the mouths of Eskimos.

Pilate's Question, Millennial Style

In a moment of high drama, the Roman governor Pontius Pilate flung a question at Jesus Christ: "What is truth?"

Jesus did not answer, or perhaps he did not have time to answer, because Pilate turned away and went out to announce that he had found no crime in Jesus (Jn 18:38). Was Pilate's question flippant? earnest? scornful? No one knows. But if Pilate were a man of today, he would ask "What is truth?" with a smirk. Then he would leave at once because he knew there was no answer, not even from Jesus.

Yet we can't really live with the idea that there's no such thing as truth. In our down-to-earth everyday lives we continue to act and talk as if there are divisions between true and false, real and phony. We embrace certain ideas because they seem genuine; we reject other ideas because our minds rebel against them as mistaken. Pushed far enough, all of us, no matter how tolerant we like to think we are, draw some lines of "either/or."

While Dale was serving on a jury in Cook County, Illinois, one of his fellow jurors showed up carrying a tote bag with the saying quoted at the beginning of this chapter: "I've given up finding the truth, just give me a good illusion." The irony of the saying apparently escaped the juror. But she would have thrown away that bag in an instant if she were ever falsely accused of a crime. She would pray that the twelve people on her jury had a consuming preference for truth over illusion.

How Do You Decide?

During a Bible study in our home a very intelligent woman whom Sandy admired greatly, vice-president and academic dean of a private college, became uncomfortable at some reference to sin as rebellion against the will of God. She thought we should be more tolerant of differing opinions about God's will. Later that week Sandy had an opportunity to talk with her about her reaction. Since this woman didn't like the way we had drawn certain lines, Sandy asked her how she told the difference between truth and falsehood or between right and wrong. She looked uncharacteristically mystified and answered, "I've never thought in those terms."

Sandy's mind stumbled at the thought of working every day in higher education while having no epistemology—that is, no criterion for deciding which knowledge is true versus which knowledge is false. We noticed, however, that this same person grew indignant when her own views about God were challenged. If we referred to God as "he" or said that Jesus was the highest revelation of God, she let us know beyond doubt that we had stepped over a line and we were, if not morally wrong, at least very mistaken.

Absolutely Nonabsolute

Critics of Christianity back themselves into a corner when they say things like "All truth is relative." Once you say "All truth is _____"—fill in the blank—you have made an absolute statement which you regard as absolutely true (and think others should regard as absolutely true). The negative statement "There's no such thing as absolute truth" is equally absolute and self-contradictory.

Yes, critics answer impatiently, but isn't the sacredness of noncontradiction a doctrine of an earlier time? Even the laws of natural science are being revolutionized by new paradigms. When fuzzy logic rules the computer world, when the line between physical reality and virtual reality is undefinable, when Gary Kasparov says the computer Deep Blue has started playing chess as if it can *think,* then contradiction has become the norm. If that's how it is in the world of technology, isn't it more so in the mystical world of religion?

Either/Or Logic

While giving a series of lectures on the Christian faith, Dr. Ravi Zacharias, born in India with ancestors in the Hindu priesthood, found himself in the odd position of being told he did not understand the workings of the Eastern mind.

During a lecture on "Why I Am a Christian," Dr. Zacharias established the law of noncontradiction: "If a statement is absolutely contradictory, without qualification, that statement cannot be true." He then explained that he concludes Hinduism is untrue because it is "plagued by contradiction."

The next day Dr. Zacharias had lunch with a professor of philosophy, an American who "had adopted the Eastern mystical worldview for himself and was most agitated that I, an Indian, had committed my life to Christ."

The professor began, "Your biggest problem is that you do not understand Eastern logic," and went on at length explaining that the Western way of looking at reality uses "either/or" logic while the Eastern way uses "both/and" logic. In Eastern thought, the professor said, contradiction is no problem.

Dr. Zacharias asked if he might interrupt his companion's train of thought and raise a question.

I said, "Sir, are you telling me that when I am studying Hinduism I either use the both/and system of logic or nothing else?"

There was a pin-drop silence for what seemed an eternity. I repeated my question: "Are you telling me that when I am studying Hinduism I either use the both/and logic or nothing else? Have I got that right?"

He threw his head back and said, "The either/or does seem to emerge, doesn't it?"

"Indeed, it does emerge," I said. "And as a matter of fact, even in India we look both ways before we cross the street— it is either the bus or me, not both of us."

"He was using the either/or logic in order to prove the both/and," Dr. Zacharias explains. "The more you try to hammer the law of noncontradiction, the more it hammers you."[4]

In fairness to Hinduism we asked a devout young Hindu, an Indian studying in this country, to critique this chapter with particular attention to what Ravi Zacharias had to say. He responded that the self-contradictions of Hinduism "came out only when Western philosophers began analyzing Eastern thought. We don't think of it as a contradiction. In Hindu religion, the most perfect and spiritually advanced person would be an ascetic because asceticism, doing without the things needed for life, is a contradiction to life."

Nothing But Mythology?

Contradiction didn't bother mythologist Joseph Campbell, who became well known through his television conversations with Bill Moyers. In an earlier book Campbell had betrayed his mind about the unreality of religions. Campbell's viewpoint, toned down in the Moyers interviews, was that all religions are nothing but mythology, divorced from any objective reality. Mortimer Adler writes that for Joseph Campbell (and we might add for many other analysts of religion),

> none of the world's organized and institutional religions, especially those that are explicitly credal, is anything but a mythology, and none has either truth or falsity in the logical sense of these terms. . . .
>
> Those with religious faith who think their own religion is not a mythology, as other people's religions are, make the mistake of thinking that their beliefs have logical truth. Asserted as facts rather than as fiction, all religious beliefs are, in logical terms, false. To be more precise, the judgment asserting as true any religious belief about matters of fact is incorrect.[5]

Campbell's view neatly solves the problem of religious pluralism. The world's religions are all equally true in people's imaginations and all equally false in the real world. In that case there's no point in asking which religion is right except in the most subjective sense—which one is right for me right now? We can discuss which religion is most ancient or most comforting or most spectacular in its ceremonies, but we can't talk meaningfully about which one is true.

As an adherent of no religion, Joseph Campbell was not the person to speak with authority about any religion. The annoying fact, which he attempted to sweep away, is that, from the inside, all religions claim to teach exclusive truths. Why else are Judaism, Christianity and Islam, all springing from the same monotheistic roots, unable to completely accept one another? Even Baha'i, supposedly a blending of all religions, makes the exclusive truth claim that all religions teach the same thing.

Since all religions are arrogant enough to claim they have the truth, we have to take on the question of whether the Christian claim to truth is backed up by anything more than the opinions of its adherents.

The Truth Is a Person
Pilate's question "What is truth?" can never be wholly answered in this life. Even when we find a partial answer, it is seldom convenient to follow the answer where it leads. Christians believe the question cannot be answered at all unless God takes the initiative to reveal his truth. But Christians believe the truth is there. Not only "out there," as a popular television show says, but here—confronting us in everyday life, revealed by God to ordinary fallible human beings on this damaged earth.

We even believe that our Lord claimed to *be* the truth when he said "I am the way and the truth and the life" (Jn 14:6). For Christians, truth is not an abstract concept but is a Person, Jesus Christ. That Person can be known—and there is a cost as well as a reward for personally knowing and following the Truth.

Easy to Accept?
Recently we loaned a friend a book presenting the case for Christianity.

He just wrote to say that he can accept the Old and New Testaments as basic guides for behavior, "human to human," but his mind still gets in the way of accepting them in their entirety as "gospel truths."

The same day we got that letter, we put up a roll of paper towels in the kitchen and discovered that the print on them is a cartoon of Noah's ark. In its typical cartoon version this is an outlandish-sounding tale: an old man rounds up pairs of all the animals in the world, puts them on a giant boat and rides out a global flood! Our friend has a point. It's easier to accept the moral teachings of the Bible than to accept some of its stories.

Or is it? The moral teachings of the Bible clash with how most of us find it convenient and comfortable to live. To love God above all else . . . to love our enemies . . . to be satisfied with what God provides and refrain from coveting what others have . . . to be faithful to one marriage partner for life or to be celibate . . . The moral teachings of the Bible get tougher the more we read them.

Before we consider whether Christianity is true, we have to ask: Am I *willing* for it to be true? To accept it is to accept the possibility that my life needs to change and to invite God to make those changes. Here the intellect can conflict with the will. We discover it's not enough to agree mentally that certain facts are true. We must follow those facts to a Person and follow that Person to the end.

Jesus never asks us to agree; he asks us to join up, to *follow*. He did not call for cognitive assent; he asked for a life of discipleship involving the whole self, not just the mind. . . . We Christians really would have no idea what the truth is if it were not for our being met and called by Jesus.[6]

We have to qualify that statement by saying that Jesus did not call for *only* cognitive assent; he does ask us to learn about him and accept him with our minds. Still we have to agree with the Christian apologist Josh McDowell, who for years has presented arguments for Christianity on university campuses. McDowell finds that "the rejection of Christ is often not so much of the 'mind,' but of the 'will'; not so much 'I can't,' but 'I won't.'"[7] Some of the most intelligent people have decided with the will that they won't.

Red, Pink, Gray and Black

The Jesus Seminar, which became famous through its own publicity campaign, meets twice a year "to vote on the historical accuracy of the sayings attributed to Jesus in the Gospels." The 74 Fellows[8] of the Jesus Seminar vote on each saying of Jesus via colored ballots: red if they think Jesus really said it; pink if he said something like it; gray if he had ideas like it but the statement isn't his; and black if the statement was added later by somebody else. The Fellows judge Jesus' words from the premise of guilty until proven innocent. "All sayings, it is assumed, are black unless they can be 'proven' to be a different hue."[9]

Not surprisingly, 82 percent of the sayings of Jesus in the four Gospels have been voted against by the Seminar as not authentically the words of Jesus. The Fellows assume that all the stories of Jesus doing miracles, claiming to be divine, dying for sins or rising from the dead were added later by a church which exaggerated and mythologized their dead leader. Their assumption shows no interest in the historic evidence for the Jesus who really lived.

John Dominic Crossan, who cofounded the Jesus Seminar with Robert W. Funk in 1985, states their purpose bluntly: "We want to liberate Jesus. The only Jesus most people know is the mythic one. They don't want the real Jesus, they want the one they can worship. The cultic Jesus."[10]

Who is this "real Jesus" the Seminar wants to liberate? In the words of one critic, he is "a warm, fuzzy counterculture guru"[11] who has been remade in the image of his reinterpreters. Purged of his divinity by a group of middle-aged, left-leaning armchair theologians, Jesus ends up sounding remarkably like a middle-aged, left-leaning armchair theologian.

Since Miracles Can't Happen . . .

The skepticism of the Jesus Seminar is nothing new. In the nineteenth century theologians commonly assumed that the New Testament was written or else rewritten during the second to fifth centuries A.D. Their logic was that the Gospels attribute numerous miracles to Jesus, and since miracles can't happen, the divine elements must have been added later as various legends grew up around the stories of Jesus the moral teacher.

What was operating in nineteenth-century biblical criticism, and what is operating in the Jesus Seminar, is not a desire to get to the truth; it's a philosophical prejudice against what the Bible overtly and clearly says. The critics first determine what the original New Testament books could *not* have said (that Jesus did miracles, rose from the dead, claimed to be the Son of God), then assign all statements which don't fit their prejudice to the category of later additions or editing. Historically, however, we have good reason to believe that what appears in our New Testaments today is what appeared in the original manuscripts written by people who knew Jesus or who knew the apostles. In fact, compared with the evidence for other ancient writings which are accepted without question, the evidence for New Testament accuracy is overwhelming.

Tough and Risky Words

When Christians claim that our faith is true, we mean more than that our book presents the facts about Jesus accurately. We mean that our Lord is real and alive, not a symbol or a legend or a dead hero.

The apostle Paul wrote bluntly to the Corinthian church that "if Christ has not been raised, your faith is futile; you are still in your sins" (1 Cor 15:17). Those are tough words, risky for Paul to send by courier from Ephesus when he couldn't see his readers' reactions. He was telling the Corinthians that if Christ's supposed resurrection of about twenty years earlier turned out to be a hoax, their salvation was a hoax also.

Risky as it is, Christians are willing to stake the truth or falsehood of our faith in Jesus Christ on whether or not he rose from the dead. Many Christian writers have put it in uncompromising terms:

The Christian faith, although it is a whole system, can be completely decimated in principle if one can fully establish that Jesus did not rise from the dead.[12]

The first fact in the history of Christendom is a number of people who say they have seen the Resurrection. If they had died without making anyone else believe this "gospel" no Gospels would ever have been written.[13]

Both friends and enemies of the Christian faith have recognized the

resurrection of Christ to be the foundation stone of the Faith. . . . [I]f
Christ did *not* rise from the dead, Christianity is an interesting museum
piece—nothing more.[14]

Beginning with the Roman and Jewish leaders, there have been many
people with a stake in proving that Jesus did not rise from the dead.
Concerning that endeavor, Ravi Zacharias wrote:

Many have tried to do just that and have either turned to Christ
themselves in the process or have abandoned their attempt at dis-
proof as an utter failure. No one in history could have wanted to
disprove the resurrection more than the temple authorities or the
Roman hierarchy. In subsequent years, no force would have wanted
to rob Christianity of that claim more than Islam did. Yet the truth
stands tall.[15]

Some reply that in Jesus' day people were unscientific and naive and were
prepared to believe in miracles. We can only refer to how Jesus' closest
followers reacted to the first news of his resurrection: though it was their
greatest hope and wish, they didn't believe it. (See Lk 24 and Jn 20.) They
knew as well as we do that people who endure death by torture do not
reappear alive and well after being buried for three days.

But Isn't It Still Arrogant?

There is still an accusation hanging in the air: Isn't it arrogant for
Christians to say they are *the* ones who have *the* truth when all religions
claim to have the truth? Do Christians think they're the only ones God
talks to? Hasn't God spoken to all people?

The Bible agrees that yes, God has spoken to all people.

The Old Testament, written by and for the Jewish nation, still acknowledges that God reveals himself throughout the world to Jew and Gentile:

The heavens declare the glory of God;
    the skies proclaim the work of his hands.
Day after day they pour forth speech;
    night after night they display knowledge.
There is no speech or language
    where their voice is not heard.

Their voice goes out into all the earth,
>   their words to the ends of the world.
(Ps 19:1-4)

Jesus, the Jewish Messiah, was very open to touching and accepting Gentiles as his followers. At times he praised the faith of Gentiles in contrast with the faithlessness of Jewish religious leaders (for example, the Roman centurion in Lk 7:1-10 and the Samaritan leper in Lk 17:11-19).

The Christian church in its earliest days was made up of Jews who believed in Jesus. When God revealed to the apostle Peter that salvation was for all people, the church reluctantly but definitely responded by accepting Gentile believers as Christians (Acts 10—11; 15).

The apostle Paul, who unapologetically called Jesus Christ the "one mediator" between God and humanity (1 Tim 2:5), also wrote that people worldwide know what God wants, although they rebel against it—

> For what can be known about God is plain to them, because God has shown it to them. For since the creation of the world his eternal power and divine nature, invisible though they are, have been understood and seen through the things he has made. So they are without excuse. (Rom 1:19-20 NRSV)

A learned man steeped in the Jewish Law, Paul could still write the remarkable words that non-Jews had God's law "written on their hearts":

> Indeed, when Gentiles, who do not have the law, do by nature things required by the law, they are a law for themselves, even though they do not have the law, since they show that the requirements of the law are written on their hearts, their consciences also bearing witness, and their thoughts now accusing, now even defending them. (Rom 2:14-15)

The Way Back

The problem is not that people lack knowledge of God. The problem is what we have done with that knowledge—*we,* including Christians, including people of all religions and no religion and halfway between religions. Something is broken in our relationship with our Creator. We are not where we should be in relation to this God who made us.

Then the vital question for all of us is: What does this God require in order to mend the relationship? How do we—any of us of any color or language or religious background—get back to God?

Christians believe that God has revealed what he requires. First, we must acknowledge our own responsibility for the separation. We have willfully rebelled against our own Creator. We cannot repair the damage. We cannot—much as we want to, much as we try to—make it right. If anything is going to be done about the brokenness, it will have to be done by the all-powerful and all-wise God whom we have offended. We can only trust in what God has mercifully done to make things right.

Christians believe that "in Christ God was reconciling the world to himself, not counting their trespasses against them, and entrusting the message of reconciliation to us" (2 Cor 5:19 NRSV). What God mercifully did for humanity was terrible for God himself. In Jesus he became a human being and offered his own life to pay for humanity's sins. "He himself bore our sins in his body on the tree [the cross], so that we might die to sins and live for righteousness; by his wounds you have been healed" (1 Peter 2:24).

> Once you were alienated from God and were enemies in your minds because of your evil behavior. But now he has reconciled you by Christ's physical body through death to present you holy in his sight, without blemish and free from accusation. (Col 1:21-22)

Christians are called arrogant for believing that God has provided only "one way" to be saved from sin. But when we take communion and remember Jesus' flesh and blood, we are humbled and astonished—not arrogant—to think that God provided any way at all. We did not deserve it. No one does. We have only put faith in what Christ has done, and we invite other people to do the same.

If They Haven't Heard

Then if everyone is already forgiven by the death of Christ, why do Christians think they have to go convert people? As we recently heard a Christian ask, Why should one person be saved just because he or she had the advantage of being born in a certain place and educated a certain way, while another person never gets that chance?

It's a question which has hung around the fringes of missions since the beginning. Missionaries say, "We go because people deserve the chance to hear." But do people need to hear in order to receive the benefit of the forgiveness Christ bought? Couldn't a person out in the jungle decide that rebelling against the supreme God is no good, realize that human effort is powerless to reach God, and put faith in the supreme God to heal the broken connection?

Don Richardson, the missionary we met in chapter six, has done extensive research on indigenous religious beliefs both in his own remarkable experience and throughout the history of missions. Richardson reports the consistent phenomenon—and other missionaries have told us this firsthand—that when Christian missionaries arrive in a culture that has had no previous contact with Christianity, the nationals often act as if they were expecting the missionaries. They identify the Christian God with a supreme "sky-God" they have known about from ancient times but with whom they have tragically lost touch through some long-ago failing.

One of the amazing characteristics of this benign, omnipotent "sky-god" of mankind's many folk religions is His propensity to identify Himself with the God of Christianity! For "sky-god," though regarded in most folk religions as remote and more or less unreachable, tends to draw near and speak to folk religionists whenever—unknown to themselves—they are about to meet emissaries of the Christian God! . . . He takes pains to make it very clear that He Himself is none other than the very God those particular foreigners proclaim![16]

The phenomenon Richardson talks about has an ancient example in the book of Acts. Chapter ten tells about a Roman centurion named Cornelius who was "devout and God-fearing," generous and a person who prayed regularly. He had a vision telling him to send for someone named Simon Peter. While his servants were on the way to get Peter, Peter had his own vision telling him that he should not consider Gentiles impure or unclean. When Cornelius's servants arrived, Peter gave them lodging and willingly went with them the next day. There he found waiting Cornelius and "a large gathering of people." Cornelius announced, "We are all here in the presence of God to listen to everything the Lord has commanded you to tell us." Peter explained the gospel, and Cornelius and his household became believers. God had prepared both Cornelius and Peter for the encounter.

The story of Cornelius and the experiences of missionaries indicate how God responds to people whose knowledge is incomplete but whose hearts are hungry for the true God.

What Comes Next?

In all seven of our "myths" about Christianity, including this final one that "Christians are arrogant," there is some element of truth. Some Christians are arrogant. Some Christians have made their faith into an exclusive club. But God's forgiveness always reaches out to be inclusive, touching everyone who acknowledges need and responds in faith to his mercy.

What next? Anyone who has been hurt by Christians' arrogance will need to summon extra courage and open-mindedness in order to take another serious look at Christianity.

Examine your own heart. Are you willing not only to look at Christian faith but to find it true and begin to live by it?

Examine the heart of Christian belief. Don't just accept somebody else's version by hearsay—look at the Bible for yourself. What does it teach? The Gospel of John and the book of Romans might be good places to start or to refresh and clarify your understanding.

Examine the credibility of Christianity. Investigate the evidence, perhaps beginning with the books mentioned under "Further Resources" at the back of this book.

There is one more step to take. No matter how much a person studies and weighs Christianity, there is still the need to decide personally—will I trust myself to this Person or not? Will I say no despite all evidence and persuasion? Or will I put my faith in Jesus and commit myself to following him, not as a great teacher from the past but as my own living Savior and Lord?

Notes

Chapter 1: "Christians Force Their Morality on Others"

[1]Barbara Kantrowitz et al., "Teenagers and AIDS," *Newsweek,* Aug. 3, 1992, p. 47.

[2]Section 118.019(3) of 1985 Wisconsin Act 56.

[3]Jill Smolowe, "Outfoxing the Right," *Time,* July 10, 1995, p. 38.

[4]Claudia Dreifus, "TV's Watchdog from Tupelo," *TV Guide,* Sept. 5, 1992, pp. 11-12.

[5]Melissa Healy, "Churches Filling Void for More Young Adults," Duluth *News-Tribune,* Nov. 24, 1996, p. 12A.

[6]Michael Lewis, "Crucifixation," *The New Republic,* July 8, 1996, p. 22.

[7]John B. Judis, "Crosses to Bear," *The New Republic,* Sept. 12, 1994, p. 25.

[8]Sydney E. Ahlstrom, *A Religious History of the American People* (New Haven, Conn.: Yale University Press, 1972), p. 719.

[9]Jean Seligmann et al., "Condoms in the Classroom," *Newsweek,* Dec. 9, 1991, p. 61.

[10]George Will, "Gramm Candidacy Will Test Nation," Ashland, Wisc. *Daily Press,* March 7, 1995, p. 4.

[11]See, for example, Jo McGowan, "In India, They Abort Females," *Newsweek,* Jan. 30, 1989, p. 12; and David Neff, "Abortion-Rights Boomerang," *Christianity Today,* March 17, 1989, p. 16.

[12]See, for example, Philip Elmer-DeWitt, "Snuff Porn on the Net," *Time,* Feb. 20, 1995, p. 69; and Joshua Quittner, "Home Pages for Hate," *Time,* Jan. 22, 1996, p. 69.

[13]See, for example, George Will, "America's Slide into the Sewer," *Newsweek,* July 30, 1990, p. 64.

[14]John Cloud, "Ivy League Gomorrah?" *Time,* Sept. 22, 1997, p. 70.

[15]Charles Oliver, "A Matter of Faith" (review of James Davison Hunter's *Culture Wars: The Struggle to Define America*), *Reason,* May 1992, p. 57.

[16]George Will, "Policing a Chicago Enclave," *Newsweek,* May 17, 1993, p. 76.

[17]Joe Klein, "Whose Values?" *Newsweek,* June 8, 1992, p. 22.

[18]Maxine Schnall, *Limits: A Search for New Values* (New York: Clarkson N. Potter, 1981), p. 74.

[19]W. E. Vine, *An Expository Dictionary of New Testament Words* (London: Oliphants, 1940), 2:242.

[20]Charles Colson, "Secular Orthodoxy and Other Oxymorons," *Jubilee,* June 1989, p. 7.

[21]Charles Colson, "Trouble in the School Yard," *Jubilee,* April 1989, p. 7 (emphasis added).

[22]Merrill Harmin and Sidney B. Simon, "Values," in *Readings in Values Clarification,* ed. Sidney B. Simon and Howard Kirschenbaum (Minneapolis: Winston Press, 1973), pp. 19-20.

[23]Ibid., p. 5.

[24]Ibid., p. 11.

[25]Ibid.

[26]Barbara Ehrenreich, "Teach Diversity—with a Smile," *Time*, April 8, 1991, p. 84.

[27]Richard Bernstein, *Dictatorship of Virtue* (New York: Alfred A. Knopf, 1994), pp. 6-7 (emphasis added).

[28]Jerry Adler et al., "Taking Offense," *Newsweek*, Dec. 24, 1990, p. 48.

[29]George Will, "Curdled Politics on Campus," *Newsweek*, May 6, 1991, p. 72.

[30]Dinesh D'Souza, *Illiberal Education: The Politics of Race and Sex on Campus* (New York: Vintage Books, 1992), pp. 79-80.

[31]Adler, "Taking Offense," p. 49.

[32]Francis Schaeffer, *The Church at the End of the Twentieth Century* (London: Norfolk Press, 1970), p. 40.

[33]Bill Jack, "The First Amendment Works for Christians Too," *Christian Herald*, Sept. 1988, pp. 16, 18.

[34]Fran Sciacca, *Generation at Risk* (Minneapolis: WorldWide Publications, 1990), pp. 110-13.

Chapter 2: "Christianity Suppresses Women"

[1]Elizabeth A. Clark, *Women in the Early Church* (Collegeville, Minn.: Liturgical Press, 1983), p. 158.

[2]Ruth A. Tucker and Walter Liefeld, *Daughters of the Church: Women and Ministry from New Testament Times to the Present* (Grand Rapids, Mich.: Zondervan, 1987), p. 166.

[3]Vern L. Bullough, *The Subordinate Sex: A History of Attitudes Toward Women* (Urbana: University of Illinois Press, 1973), p. 98.

[4]Tucker and Liefeld, *Daughters of the Church*, p. 205.

[5]Barbara J. MacHaffie, *Her Story: Women in Christian Tradition* (Philadelphia: Fortress Press, 1986), pp. 75-76.

[6]Bullough, *The Subordinate Sex*, p. 22.

[7]Ibid., p. 139.

[8]Frances Gies and Joseph Gies, *Women in the Middle Ages* (New York: Thomas Y. Crowell, 1978), p. 17.

[9]Ibid., p. 20.

[10]Ibid., pp. 230-31.

[11]Michael S. Lawson, "Look Who's Going to Seminary," *Christianity Today*, Feb. 3, 1997, pp. 109, 111.

[12]Kari Torjesen Malcolm, *Women at the Crossroads: A Path Beyond Feminism and Traditionalism* (Downers Grove, Ill.: InterVarsity Press, 1982), p. 112.

[13]Ibid., p. 113.

[14]Ibid., pp. 113-14.

[15]Tucker and Liefeld, *Daughters of the Church*, p. 282.

[16]Ibid., pp. 264-65.

[17]Ibid., pp. 265-66.

[18]Ibid., p. 80, quoting Flora Larson, *My Best Men Are Women* (London: Hodder & Stoughton, 1974), p. 22.

[19]Ibid., p. 286, quoting B. T. Roberts, *Ordaining Women* (Rochester, N. Y.: Earnest Christian, 1891), p. 159.

[20]Ibid., p. 249.

[21]Wendy Murray Zoba, "The Grandmother of Us All," *Christianity Today,* Sept. 16, 1996, p. 44.

[22]Ibid., p. 46.

[23]Ruth A. Tucker, *From Jerusalem to Irian Jaya: A Biographical History of Christian Missions* (Grand Rapids, Mich.: Zondervan, 1983), p. 232.

[24]Malcolm, *Women at the Crossroads,* p. 145.

[25]Tucker, *From Jerusalem to Irian Jaya,* pp. 232-33.

[26]Robert McAfee Brown, *Unexpected News: Reading the Bible with Third World Eyes* (Philadelphia: Westminster Press, 1984), p. 25.

[27]Kenneth L. Woodward, "Feminism and the Churches," *Newsweek,* Feb. 13, 1989, p. 60.

[28]Dorothy R. Pape, *In Search of God's Ideal Woman: A Personal Examination of the New Testament* (Downers Grove, Ill.: InterVarsity Press, 1976), p. 91.

[29]Craig S. Keener, *The IVP Bible Background Commentary: New Testament* (Downers Grove, Ill.: InterVarsity Press, 1993), p. 447.

[30]Clark, *Women in the Early Church,* p. 75.

[31]Ibid.

[32]Don Williams, *The Apostle Paul and Women in the Church* (Van Nuys, Calif.: BIM Publishing, 1977), p. 54.

[33]Pape, *In Search of God's Ideal Woman,* p. 291.

[34] Vine, *An Expository Dictionary of New Testament Words,* 1:90.

[35]"Ministering Women," *Christianity Today,* April 8, 1996, p. 16.

[36]J. Daniel Lupton, *I Like Church, But . . .* (Shippensburg, Pa.: Destiny Image, 1996), p. 78.

[37]Robert Johnston, Jean Lambert, David Scholer and Klyne Snodgrass, *A Biblical and Theological Basis for Women in Ministry* (Chicago: Covenant Publications, 1987), p. 1.

Chapter 3: "Christianity Caused the Ecological Crisis"

[1]Lynn White Jr., *Science,* March 10, 1967, pp. 1203-7.

[2]Ibid., *Teleology* is a theological word from the Greek *telos* or "end." It has to do with purpose, maturity, perfection and completeness. Christians use the word to talk about events which will happen at the end of time.

[3]For example, see E. Calvin Beisner, *Prospects for Growth: A Biblical View of Population, Resources and the Future* (Westchester, Ill.: Crossway, 1990).

[4]For example, see Berit Kjos, *Under the Spell of Mother Earth* (Wheaton, Ill.: Victor Books, 1992).

[5]Yi-fu Tuan, "Our Treatment of the Environment in Ideal and Actuality," *American Scientist* 58: 248.

[6]Arthur Wood, "The Intimacy of Jesus with Nature," *London Quarterly & Holborn Review* 189 (1964): 45.

[7]Jacques Ellul, *The Technological Society,* trans. John Wilkinson (New York: Alfred A. Knopf, 1964), p. 34.

[8]Information from Joseph K. Sheldon, "Twenty-one Years After 'The Historical Roots of Our Ecologic Crisis': How Has the Church Responded?" (unpublished).

[9]Francis A. Schaeffer, *How Should We Then Live?* (Old Tappan, N.J.: Revell, 1976), p. 121.

Chapter 4: "Christians Are Antiscientific"

[1]Rowland Nethaway, "Life on Mars May Confound Religions," Duluth *News-Tribune,* Aug. 11, 1996, p. 14.

[2]Wayne W. Carley, "In Defense of Fundamentalism," *The American Biology Teacher,* 58 (April 1996): 196-97.

[3]Michael D. Lemonick, "Dumping on Darwin," *Time,* March 18, 1996, p. 81.

[4]Hugh Ross, *The Fingerprint of God* (Orange, Calif.: Promise Publishing, 1989), p. 14.

[5]Charles E. Hummel, *The Galileo Connection : Resolving Conflicts Between Science and the Bible* (Downers Grove, Ill.: InterVarsity Press, 1986), p. 119.

[6]Ross, *The Fingerprint of God,* p. 27.

[7]J. P. Moreland, "Is Science a Threat or Help to Faith?" *The Real Issue,* Nov.-Dec. 1994, p. 11 (reprinted from *Christian Research Journal,* Fall 1993).

[8]"NABT Unveils New Statement on Teaching Evolution," *The American Biology Teacher,* Jan. 1996, p. 61.

[9]Ibid., p. 62 (emphasis added).

[10]Phillip E. Johnson, *Reason in the Balance* (Downers Grove, Ill.: InterVarsity Press, 1995), p. 10.

[11]Randy Moore, "Psychics Agree! Creationism Is a Science!" *The American Biology Teacher,* 57 (April 1995):196.

[12]Stephen J. Gould, *Ever Since Darwin* (New York: W. W. Norton, 1977), p. 15.

[13]David M. Raup, *The Nemesis Affair* (New York: W. W. Norton, 1986), p. 13.

[14]Ibid., p. 196.

[15]Ibid., pp. 193-94.

[16]Leslie H. Allen, ed., *Bryan and Darrow at Dayton* (New York: Russell & Russell, 1967), p. 1.

[17]Ibid., p. 2.

[18]Ibid., pp. 112-32.

[19]Ibid., p. 133.

[20]David Goetz, "The Monkey Trial," *Christian History* 16, no. 3 (Issue 55, 1997): 10.

[21]Allen, *Bryan and Darrow at Dayton,* p. 156.

[22]Goetz, "The Monkey Trial," p. 10.

[23]Jerome Lawrence and Robert E. Lee, *Inherit the Wind* (New York: Random House/Bantam Books, 1960), p. 115.

[24]Moreland, "Is Science a Threat or Help to Faith?" p. 12.

[25]Hugh Siefken, "Faith in the Physics Lab," *Greenville College Record,* Spring 1996, p. 6.

[26]Ibid., p. 7.

[27]Ibid.

[28]Ibid.

[29]Ross, *The Fingerprint of God,* p. 76 (emphasis added).

[30]Michio Kaku, "What Happened Before the Big Bang?" *Astronomy* 24, no. 5 (May 1996): 38 (emphasis added).

[31]Kaku, p. 36 (emphasis added).

[32]Paul M. Anderson, "A Common Thread," in *Professors Who Believe: The Spiritual Journeys of Christian Faculty,* ed., Paul M. Anderson (Downers Grove, Ill.: InterVarsity Press, in press).

[33]Ibid.

[34]Carley, "In Defense of Fundamentalism," pp. 196-97.

[35]J. A. Thompson, *The Bible and Archaeology*, 3rd. ed. (Grand Rapids, Mich.: Eerdmans, 1982), p. 435.

[36]Hershel Shanks, "Fingerprints of Jeremiah's Scribe," *Biblical Archaeology Review* 22, no. 2 (March-April 1996): 36-38.

[37]Zvi Greenhut, "Burial Cave of the Caiaphas Family," *Biblical Archaeology Review* 18, no. 5 (Sept.-Oct. 1992): 28-36.

[38]"'David' Found at Dan," *Biblical Archaeology Review* 20, no. 2 (March-April 1994): 26-39.

[39]Allen, *Bryan and Darrow at Dayton*, p. 163.

Chapter 5: "Christians Have Done Terrible Things in the Name of Christ"

[1]Gordon Hilsman, Spiritual Distress Workshop, Memorial Medical Center, Ashland, Wisc., Oct. 30, 1986.

[2]David Kallas, "Obscene Lyrics," Ashland, Wisc., *Daily Press*, May 18, 1990, Northern View section, p. 3.

[3]"The Awful Truth About Church History," on "Atheist Express" home page http://www.hti.net/www/atheism/chu_hist.html

[4]Robert G. Clouse, "Flowering: The Western Church" in *Eerdmans' Handbook to the History of Christianity*, Tim Dowley et al., eds. (Grand Rapids, Mich.: Eerdmans, 1977), 271.

[5]Justo L. Gonzalez, *The Story of Christianity* (San Francisco: HarperCollins, 1984), vol. 1, p. 293.

[6]John Clare, "The Crusades," in *Eerdmans' Handbook*, p. 269.

[7]Gonzalez, *The Story of Christianity*, p. 292.

[8]Ibid., p. 293.

[9]Ibid., p. 296.

[10]Clare, "The Crusades," p. 269.

[11]Ronald Finucane, "Persecution and Inquisition," in *Eerdmans' Handbook*, pp. 314, 316.

[12]Ibid., pp. 318, 321.

[13]Ibid., p. 321.

[14]Henry Charles Lea, *A History of the Inquisition of the Middle Ages* (New York: Harper & Brothers, 1900), vol. 1, p. 52.

[15]Jacob Grimm, *Teutonic Mythology*, 4th ed., tr. James Steven Stallybrass (New York: Dover Publications, 1966) (orig. pub. George Bell and Sons, 1883), vol. 3, pp. 1065-66.

[16]Arthur Miller, *Timebends: A Life* (New York: Harper & Row, 1987), pp. 339-40.

[17]Ibid., p. 337. Pages 330-42 give Miller's full account of his research into the Salem witchcraft trials.

[18]Carol F. Karlsen, *The Devil in the Shape of a Woman* (New York: Vintage Books, 1989) p. 152.

[19]Peter Grey, *Age of Enlightenment* (New York: Time Inc., 1966), p. 11.

[20]Jerome Blum, Rondo Cameron and Thomas G. Barnes, *The European World: A History*, 2nd ed. (Boston: Little, Brown, 1970), p. 483.

[21]Francis A. Schaeffer, *How Should We Then Live?* (Old Tappan, N.J.: Revell, 1976), p. 155.

[22]Keith Michael Baker, ed., *The Old Regime and the French Revolution* (Chicago: University of Chicago Press, 1987), p. 384.

[23]Ibid., pp. 386-87.

[24]Ibid., p.385.

[25]Schaeffer, *How Should We Then Live?* p. 124.

[26]Karl Marx and Friedrich Engels, *The Communist Manifesto*, Samuel H. Beer, ed. (New York: Appleton-Century-Crofts, 1955), pp. 30-31.

[27]Jerome Blum, Rondo Cameron and Thomas G. Barnes, *The European World*, p. 804.

[28]Ibid., pp. 939-40.

[29]"Barmen Declaration," #885 in The Covenant Hymnal (Chicago: Covenant Publications, 1996).

[30]David Neff, "Our Extended, Persecuted Family," *Christianity Today*, April 29, 1996, 14.

[31]Michael Horowitz, "The Jews of the Twenty-first Century?" Interview by Charles Colson in *Jubilee*, Spring 1997, pp. 13-14, 17.

[32]"Perspectives," *Newsweek*, November 11, 1991, p. 15.

[33]Richard Thompson, "The Will to Power," *SCP Newsletter*, Summer 1985, p. 4.

Chapter 6: "Christian Missionaries Destroy Native Cultures"

[1]Art Davidson, *Endangered Peoples* (San Francisco, Calif.: Sierra Club Books, 1993), p. 8.

[2]Ibid., p. 44.

[3]J. Hudson Taylor, "The Call to Service," in *Perspectives on the World Christian Movement*, Ralph D. Winter and Steven C. Hawthorne, eds. (Pasadena, Calif.: William Carey Library, 1981), p. 242.

[4]William Carey, "An Enquiry into the Obligation of Christians to Use Means for the Conversion of the Heathens," in *Perspectives on the World Christian Movement*, p. 233.

[5]Don Richardson, *Eternity in Their Hearts*, rev. ed. (Ventura, Calif.: Regal, 1984), pp. 142-43.

[6]Paul Johnson, *The Birth of the Modern: World Society 1815-1830* (New York, Harper-Collins, 1991), p. 244.

[7]R. Pierce Beaver, "The History of Mission Strategy," in *Perspectives on the World Christian Movement*, p. 199.

[8]Steven J. Keillor, *This Rebellious House: American History and The Truth of Christianity* (Downers Grove, Ill.: InterVarsity Press, 1996), p. 200.

[9]Ibid., p. 221.

[10]Ruth A. Tucker, *From Jerusalem to Irian Jaya*, p. 151.

[11]Ibid., p. 104.

[12]Merrill D. Beal, *I Will Fight No More Forever: Chief Joseph and the Nez Perce War* (New York: Ballantine, 1963), p. 16.

[13]Ibid., p. 17.

[14]Ibid., p. 324.

[15]Bernard J. Lambert, *Shepherd of the Wilderness* (L'Anse, Mich.: Bernard J. Lambert, 1967), pp. 66-67, 96-101, 124-28.

[16]Ibid., pp. 62-63.

[17]Davidson, *Endangered Peoples*, p. 194.

[18]*Webster's Encyclopedic Unabridged Dictionary of the English Language* (New York:

Gramercy Books, 1989), p. 1017.

[19]Howard and Geraldine Taylor, *Hudson Taylor's Spiritual Secret* (Chicago: Moody, 1932; reprint ed., n.d.), pp. 64-65.

[20]Ibid., pp. 65-66.

[21]J. J. Ellis, *James Hudson Taylor: A Little Man Who Did Great Things for God* (London: Pickering & Inglis, n.d.), pp. 33-34.

[22]Taylor and Taylor, *Hudson Taylor's Spiritual Secret*, p. 67.

[23]Tucker, *From Jerusalem to Irian Jaya*, p. 176.

[24]Norman P. Grubb, *C. T. Studd: Cricketer and Pioneer* (London: Religious Tract Society, 1933), pp. 76-77.

[25]Alain Chenevière, *Vanishing Tribes* (New York: Doubleday, 1987), p. 27.

[26]Ibid., p. 97.

[27]Andrea Dorfman, "Lost Africa," *Time*, Sept. 2, 1996, p. 56.

[28]Ralph D. Winter and David A. Fraser, "World Mission Survey," in *Perspectives on the World Christian Movement*, pp. 341-42.

[29]Tucker, *From Jerusalem to Irian Jaya*, p. 461.

[30]Paul Hiebert, "Culture and Cross-Cultural Differences," in *Perspectives on the World Christian Movement*, p. 377.

[31]"Apology to Native Congregations—United Church of Christ," appendix C in Matthew Fox, *The Coming of the Cosmic Christ* (San Francisco: Harper & Row, 1988), pp. 249-50.

[32]"Apology to Native Congregations—United Church of Canada," appendix A in Fox, *The Coming of the Cosmic Christ*, p. 247.

[33]"Apology to Native Congregations—Pacific Northwest Church Leaders," appendix B in Fox, *The Coming of the Cosmic Christ*, pp. 247-48.

[34]Richardson, *Eternity in Their Hearts*, p. 111.

[35]Ibid.

[36]Ibid., p. 112.

[37]Ibid., p. 59.

[38]Tucker, *From Jerusalem to Irian Jaya*, p. 483.

[39]Mike Webb, "Death of the Rainforest," *Tear Times*, Autumn 1990, p. 4.

[40]Ibid., p. 6.

[41]"Global Action Network," *Tear Times*, Spring 1997, p. 11.

[42]"Niger: The Long Sleep," *Tear Times*, Winter 1995, p. 19.

[43]Ralph D. Winter, "The New Macedonia: A Revolutionary New Era in Mission Begins," in *Perspectives on the World Christian Movement*, p. 311.

Chapter 7: "Christians Are Arrogant"

[1]Mortimer J. Adler, *Truth In Religion: The Plurality of Religions and the Unity of Truth* (New York: Macmillan, 1990), p. 21 (emphasis added).

[2]Lewis Carroll, *Through the Looking-Glass* (New York: Children's Classics, 1990), pp. 102-3.

[3]Jerry Adler with Niko Price, "The Melting of the Mighty Myth," *Newsweek*, July 22, 1991, p. 63.

[4]Ravi Zacharias, *Can Man Live Without God?* (Dallas, Tex.: Word, 1994), pp. 127-29.

[5]Adler, *Truth In Religion*, p. 61.

[6]William H. Willimon, "Jesus' Peculiar Truth," *Christianity Today,* March 4, 1996, pp. 21-22.

[7]Josh McDowell, *Evidence That Demands a Verdict: Historical Evidences for the Christian Faith,* rev. ed. (San Bernardino, Calif.: Here's Life Publishers, 1979), p. 10.

[8]Most Jesus Seminar participants have scant scholarly credentials. See Robert J. Hutchinson, "The Jesus Seminar Unmasked," *Christianity Today,* April 29, 1996, pp. 28-30, reviewing Luke Timothy Johnson's book *The Real Jesus: The Mistaken Quest for the Historical Jesus and the Truth of the Traditional Gospels* (San Francisco, Calif.: Harper San Francisco, 1996).

[9]James R. Edwards, "'Who Do Scholars Say That I Am?'" *Christianity Today,* March 4, 1996, p. 15.

[10]Brad Scott, "Jesus on the Rack," *SCP Journal* 21, nos. 1-2 (1997): 27.

[11]Ibid.

[12]Zacharias, *Can Man Live Without God?* p. 113.

[13]C. S. Lewis, *Miracles: A Preliminary Study* (New York: Macmillan, 1947), p. 149.

[14]Paul E. Little, *Know Why You Believe* (Wheaton, Ill.: Victor Books, 1967), p. 41.

[15]Zacharias, *Can Man Live Without God?* p. 113.

[16]Richardson, *Eternity in Their Hearts,* p. 50.

Further Resources

Chapter 1: "Christians Force Their Morality on Others"

Gaede, S. D. *When Tolerance Is No Virtue*. Downers Grove, Ill.: InterVarsity Press, 1993.

McDowell, Josh. *Right from Wrong*. Dallas, Tex.: Word, 1994. Aimed at people working with teens.

Watkins, William D. *The New Absolutes*. Minneapolis: Bethany House, 1996.

Chapter 2: "Christianity Suppresses Women"

Grenz, Stanley, with Denise Muir Kjesbo. *Women in the Church: A Biblical Theology of Women in Ministry*. Downers Grove, Ill.: InterVarsity Press, 1995.

Malcolm, Kari Torjesen. *Women at the Crossroads: A Path Beyond Feminism & Traditionalism*. Downers Grove, Ill.: InterVarsity Press, 1982.

Tucker, Ruth A., and Walter Liefeld. *Daughters of the Church: Women and Ministry from New Testament Times to the Present*. Grand Rapids, Mich.: Zondervan, 1987.

Chapter 3: "Christianity Caused the Ecological Crisis"

Au Sable Institute, RR 2, Mancelona, MI 49659. 616-587-8686.

Evangelical Environmental Network, 10 E. Lancaster Ave., Wynnewood, PA 19096. 610-645-9392. een@esa.mhs.compuserve.com

Freudenberger, C. Dean. *Global Dust Bowl*. Minneapolis: Augsburg, 1990.

Goudzwaard, Bob. *Idols of Our Time*. Downers Grove, Ill.: InterVarsity Press, 1984.

Restoring Creation for Ecology and Justice. Louisville, Ky.: Office of the General Assembly, Presbyterian Church (USA), 1990. A sample of one denomination's statement on ecology.

Schaeffer, Francis A., with Udo Middelmann. *Pollution and the Death of Man*. Wheaton, Ill.: Crossway Books, 1992 (originally published by Tyndale House, 1970).

Van Dyke, Fred, David C. Mahan, Joseph K. Sheldon and Raymond H. Brand. *Redeeming Creation: The Biblical Basis for Environmental Stewardship*. Downers Grove, Ill.: InterVarsity Press, 1996.

Chapter 4: "Christians Are Antiscientific"

Barrett, Eric C., and David Fisher, eds. *Scientists Who Believe: 21 Tell Their Own Stories*. Chicago: Moody Press, 1984.

Behe, Michael J. *Darwin's Black Box: The Biochemical Challenge to Evolution*. New York: Free Press, 1996.

Hummel, Charles E. *The Galileo Connection : Resolving Conflicts Between Science and the Bible*. Downers Grove, Ill.: InterVarsity Press, 1986.

Johnson, Phillip. *Darwin on Trial*. 2nd ed. Downers Grove, Ill.: InterVarsity Press, 1993.

———. *Reason in the Balance: The Case Against Naturalism in Science, Law & Educa-*

tion. Downers Grove, Ill.: InterVarsity Press, 1995.

Ross, Hugh. *The Fingerprint of God.* Orange, Calif.: Promise Publishing Co., 1989.

Wright, Richard T. *Biology Through the Eyes of Faith.* San Francisco: Harper & Row Publishers, 1989.

Chapter 5: "Christians Have Done Terrible Things in the Name of Christ"

Keillor, Steven. *This Rebellious House.* Downers Grove, Ill.: InterVarsity Press, 1996.

Chapter 6: "Christian Missionaries Destroy Native Cultures"

Elliot, Elisabeth. *Shadow of the Almighty: The Life and Testament of Jim Elliot.* Grand Rapids, Mich.: Zondervan, 1958.

Richardson, Don. *Eternity in Their Hearts.* Rev. ed. Ventura, Calif.: Regal, 1984.

————. *Peace Child.* Ventura, Calif.: Regal, 1974.

Tucker, Ruth A. *From Jerusalem to Irian Jaya: A Biographical History of Christian Missions.* Grand Rapids, Mich.: Zondervan, 1983.

Winter, Ralph D., and Steven C. Hawthorne, eds. *Perspectives on the World Christian Movement.* Pasadena, Calif.: William Carey Library, 1981.

Chapter 7: "Christians Are Arrogant"

Bockmuehl, Markus. *This Jesus: Martyr, Lord, Messiah.* Downers Grove, Ill.: InterVarsity Press, 1996.

Bruce, F. F. *The New Testament Documents: Are They Reliable?* 6th ed. Grand Rapids, Mich.: Eerdmans, 1992.

Lewis, C. S. *Mere Christianity.* New York: Macmillan, 1952.

Little, Paul E. *Know Why You Believe.* Wheaton, Ill.: Victor Books, 1967.

McCallam, Dennis, gen. ed. *The Death of Truth.* Minneapolis: Bethany House, 1996.

McDowell, Josh. *Evidence That Demands a Verdict: Historical Evidence for the Christian Faith.* Rev. ed. San Bernardino, Calif.: Here's Life Publishers, 1979.

Lutzer, Erwin W. *Christ Among Other Gods.* Chicago: Moody Press, 1994.

Montgomery, John Warwick. *History and Christianity.* Minneapolis: Bethany House, 1965.

Sire, James W. *The Universe Next Door,* 3rd ed. Downers Grove, Ill.: InterVarsity Press, 1997. See especially chapter nine, "The Vanished Horizon."

Stott, John. *Basic Christianity.* 2nd ed. Downers Grove, Ill.: InterVarsity Press, 1971.

Zacharias, Ravi. *Can Man Live Without God?* Dallas, Tex.: Word, 1994.